My Dearest Allison,

May you live to experience all of this!

I love you,

Mom

'92

FRANCE
AND ITS
CUISINE

MALLARD
PRESS

RECIPES SELECTED AND EDITED BY JANE ADAMS AND JILLIAN STEWART
DESIGNED BY ALISON JEWELL AND MARNIE SEARCHWELL
JACKET DESIGN BY JUSTINE DAVIES
FOOD PHOTOGRAPHY BY PETER BARRY AND
   NEIL SUTHERLAND

MALLARD PRESS

An imprint of BDD Promotional Book Company Inc.,
666 Fifth Avenue, New York, N.Y. 10103.
Mallard Press and its accompanying design and logo
are trademarks of BDD Promotional Book Company Inc.

CLB 2370
Copyright© 1991 Colour Library Books Ltd.,
Godalming, Surrey, England.
Text filmsetting by Words and Spaces, Hampshire, England.
First published in the United States of America
in 1991 by the Mallard Press.
Printed and bound in Hong Kong.
ISBN 0 792 45227 5

FRANCE
AND ITS
CUISINE

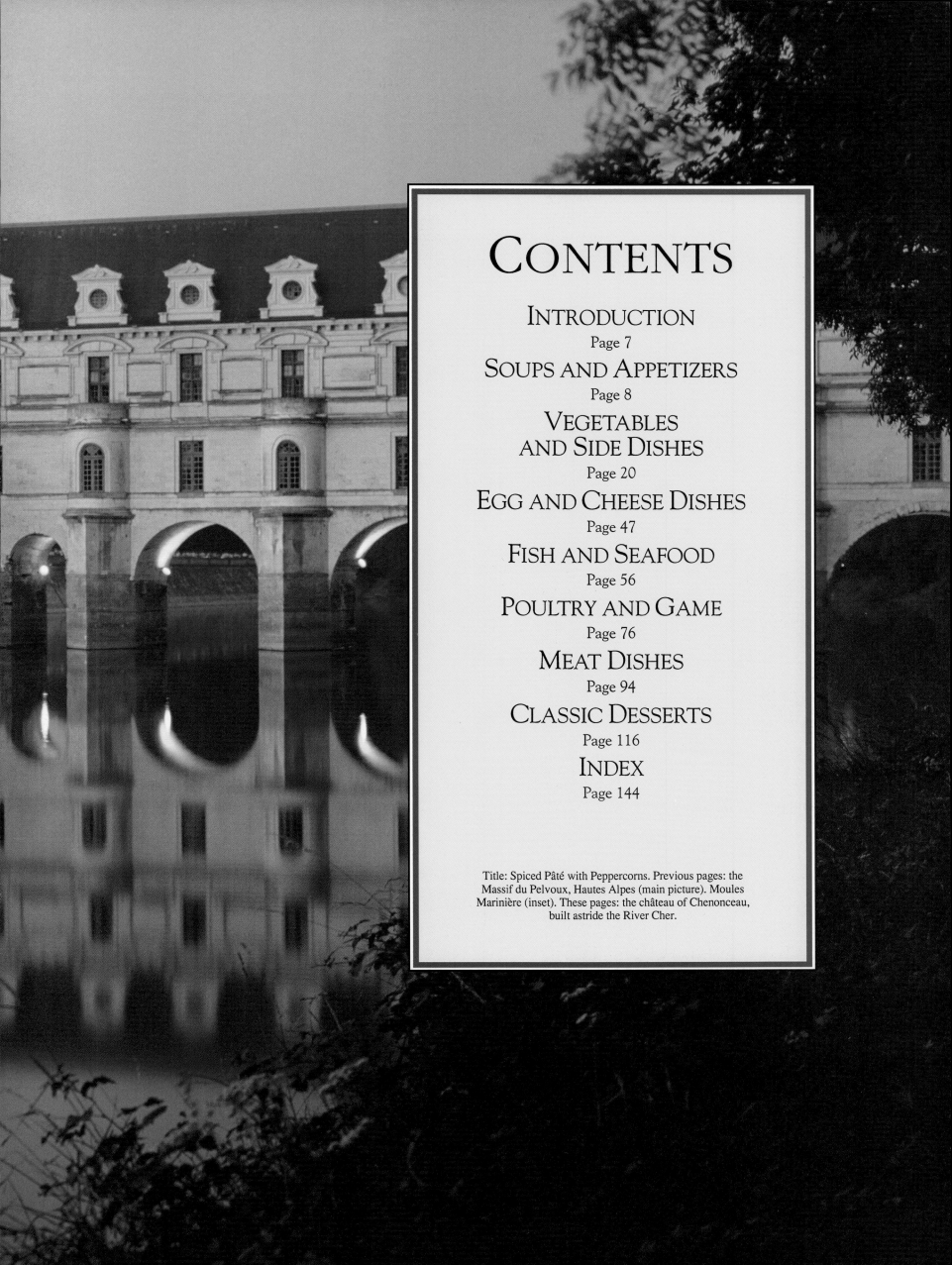

CONTENTS

Title: Spiced Pâté with Peppercorns. Previous pages: the
Massif du Pelvoux, Hautes Alpes (main picture). Moules
Marinière (inset). These pages: the château of Chenonceau,
built astride the River Cher.

INTRODUCTION

Such is the effect of classic French cuisine on those who have savored its delights that the mere mention of it sends their thoughts drifting off to a dinner table set, perhaps, in the shade of a beautiful Provençal garden or in an intimate restaurant along the Champs-Elysées in Paris. For the French style of cooking and entertaining, by combining quality and imagination, has secured itself a unique position as one of the world's most outstanding cuisines.

To understand the significance of food in France we must first understand its place in French society as both an institution and an art form — the French regard eating as one of life's great pleasures, something which is there to be enjoyed but which should also be treated with respect. Quality has always been the basis of French cuisine: the best and freshest possible ingredients are the starting point of a memorable meal. Unfortunately most people no longer have a vegetable garden of their own, so the task of seeking out the best produce available is undertaken daily, and with great gravity, in the markets of France. In the preparation and cooking of a classic French meal, technical skill is probably less important than the amount of loving care and attention to detail that the cook is willing to lavish on these ingredients.

François Pierre de La Varenne is widely recognised as France's first great chef and, as such, the forefather of modern French cuisine. It was La Varenne who, in the sixteenth century, finally dispensed with the practice of using overpowering sauces and spices. In their place he advocated the use of natural meat juices, butter and subtle sauces to enhance rather than smother the flavor of the dishes. As well as possessing immense culinary skill and imagination, La Varenne insisted on previously unheard-of standards of detail and presentation: standards which are still adhered to today.

After La Varenne, French cuisine continued to blossom under a succession of kings who were enthusiastic about their food. With increasing culinary standards, a greater emphasis on the actual organisation, preparation and serving of the meal also developed. This involved meticulous planning – finding and buying the freshest ingredients, deciding on the best wine to serve, setting out the finest tableware, and most important of all, paying the closest possible attention to the final appearance and flavor of the dishes. This attention to detail has become an irrevocable part of French cooking, a trait which has ensured its place as the most civilised and sophisticated of cuisines.

Like most culinary styles, French cooking exhibits great regional variations; many of its most famous dishes developed as a result of utilizing localized produce, and these specialties have since become an integral part of the national repertoire whilst remaining the pride of their respective regional restaurants. Thus, the coast of Brittany is acclaimed for its fish and seafood, which go to make delicious fish stews and soups. Normandy produces cream, butter, cider and Calvados (apple brandy) and a number of rich dishes that make the most of these these ingredients. Moving south, Bordeaux has its wine, of course, but is also famous for its cheeses, while Provence is one of the most beautiful of France's regions with a climate that is ideal for growing a whole variety of fruits and vegetables – it is from here that such colorful and delicious dishes as Salade Nicoise originate.

The above are just a few of the attractions of French cuisine; inside this book you will find many more. From delicious appetizers to tempting salads and divine desserts, *France and its cuisine* provides the cook with the very best recipes that France has to offer.

Standing over 900 feet high, the Eiffel Tower dominates the Paris skyline.

SERVES 6

Anchoyade

This tangy anchovy paste is spread on toast and served with drinks before a meal.

PREPARATION TIME: 25 minutes

---

15 salted anchovy fillets
½ cup olive oil
2 cloves garlic, peeled
Few drops lemon juice

TO SERVE
1 prepared lettuce
4 tbsps vinaigrette dressing
12 slices bread, toasted

Toss the lettuce in the vinaigrette dressing. Rinse the anchovy fillets under cold running water to remove the excess salt. Pat them dry on kitchen paper. Pound the garlic with a pestle and mortar until smooth. Pound the anchovy fillets into the garlic until smooth. Beat in the oil, a little at a time, until a smooth paste is formed. Spread the mixture onto the slices of toast and place them on top of the tossed lettuce.

The town hall in Calais, France's most important passenger port. The town has close ties with Britain, which is only twenty miles away.

The port and old town of Menton are situated on the very edge of the frontier
with Italy. The town is a popular haunt for visitors tired of the bustle of the
more famous Riviera resorts nearby.

SERVES 4

Potage Crème Dubarry

This creamy soup gives the humble cauliflower sophisticated status.

PREPARATION TIME: 10 minutes
COOKING TIME: 45 minutes

1 cauliflower
4 tbsps butter or margarine
1½ tbsps flour
2½ cups chicken stock
1 onion, peeled and chopped
2 medium egg yolks
⅔ cup heavy cream

Cheese, shredded
Nutmeg
Salt
Pepper

GARNISH
Snipped chives

Trim the cauliflower and break into flowerets. Cook in gently boiling salted water for 5 minutes. Drain and set aside. Melt the butter in a pan and stir in the flour. Cook for 1-2 minutes, stirring. Remove from heat and stir in the chicken stock. Add the onion, and return to the heat. Bring to the boil, stirring continuously, and then simmer for 20 minutes. Allow to cool. Add cauliflower and blend. Push through a strainer. Return soup to pan, and reheat. Lightly beat together the egg yolks, cream and a little shredded cheese to taste. Stir in some soup, and then put all of the mixture back into the pan. Cook gently until thickened, but do not let it boil. Season with salt and pepper and grated nutmeg. Garnish with snipped chives.

SERVES 6-8

Spiced Pâté with Peppercorns

This chunky pâté is French country cooking at its best. Serve it either as a substantial appetizer or, with French bread and a green salad, as a light lunch.

PREPARATION TIME: 20 minutes
COOKING TIME: 1½-2 hours

4-6oz sliced bacon, rind and bones removed
1lb lean pork, cubed
1lb veal, cubed
8oz pork fat back, cubed
3 shallots, finely chopped
¼ tsp each of powdered ginger, mace and allspice
2 tsps chopped fresh or dried tarragon
1 egg
3 tbsps brandy
1 tbsp green peppercorns, rinsed and drained if canned
Salt

Line a loaf pan with the strips of bacon, leaving the ends overlapping the edge of the dish. Combine pork, veal, pork fat back, shallots, spices, tarragon and salt in the bowl of a food processor. Work in short bursts until chopped. Do not overwork. Add the egg and brandy and process until just blended together. Stir in the peppercorns by hand. Press the mixture into the pan on top of the bacon and fold the ends of bacon over the pâté mixture. Cover tightly with aluminum foil and place pan in a roasting pan half full of hot water. Bake in a moderate oven, 350°F, for 1½-2 hours or until pâté shrinks from the sides of the pan and the juices run clear. Cool before weighting down the top and chilling in the refrigerator overnight or until firm enough to slice easily.

Wedged between rocky cliffs and the Dordogne River is the pretty village of La Roque-Gageac.

SERVES 4

Chicken Liver Pâté

Serve this rich, smooth pâté with delicate Melba toast for an elegant appetizer.

PREPARATION TIME: 15 minutes
COOKING TIME: 15 minutes

---

2 tbsps butter for frying
1 clove garlic, minced
1 onion, peeled and diced finely
8oz chicken livers, trimmed
4 tbsps butter, creamed

1 tbsp brandy
Salt
Pepper

GARNISH
Dill

Heat the butter in a frying pan. Add the garlic, onions, salt, and freshly ground black pepper, and fry gently until onions have softened. Increase heat, and sauté the chicken livers in hot butter for about 2 minutes on each side, until they are just cooked through. Blend the contents of the frying pan and push through a wire strainer into a bowl using the back of a spoon. Beat in the creamed butter, and the brandy, and adjust seasoning. Place in one large dish or 4 individual custard cups. If not being eaten immediately, seal the surface with clarified butter and refrigerate. Garnish with dill.

Mont St-Michel is one of France's most popular tourist attractions. This unusual offshore mount is topped by a magnificent Gothic abbey which once attracted crowds of medieval pilgrims.

SERVES 4

Soupe de Poisson Provençale

In contrast to France's other famous fish soup, Bouillabaisse, this one is smooth and creamy, but don't let this fool you – the accompanying sauce is fiery hot.

PREPARATION TIME: 20 minutes
COOKING TIME: 30-40 minutes

SOUP
1 large onion
2 leeks
⅔ cup olive oil
2 cloves garlic
5 cups canned tomatoes
3lbs whitefish
8oz shrimp
1 bay leaf
1 sprig thyme
1 small piece fennel or 2 parsley
   stalks
Strip of orange rind
5 cups water
⅔ cup white wine
2 pinches saffron
Tomato paste
2 tbsps butter

2 tbsps flour
Cream
Salt
Pepper

SAUCE ROUILLE
1 small chili pepper
½ cup chopped red pepper or
   canned pimento
3-4 tbsps fresh breadcrumbs
3 cloves garlic
1 egg yolk
Salt
Pepper
⅔ cup olive oil

ACCOMPANIMENT
Shredded Parmesan cheese
Croûtons

First prepare the soup. Chop the onion. Clean and chop the leeks, and cook them slowly, with the onion, in the olive oil until tender, but not browned. Mince the garlic cloves and add to the leeks and onion, along with the canned tomatoes. Bring to the boil and cook for 5 minutes. Meanwhile, skin and bone the fish, shell the shrimp, and tie the bay leaf, thyme, fennel and orange peel together with a small piece of string. Put the water, wine, the bundle of herbs, the saffron, salt and pepper, fish and shellfish into the pan and cook, uncovered, on a moderate heat for 30-40 minutes. Meanwhile, prepare the rouille. Cut the chili pepper in half and rinse out seeds. Use half or all of it, depending on desired hotness. Chop the chili pepper together with sweet red pepper. Peel and chop the garlic. Soak breadcrumbs in water and press them dry. Put peppers, breadcrumbs, garlic and egg yolk into a blender with a pinch of salt and pepper and blend to a smooth paste, or work together with mortar and pestle. Gradually add the oil in a thin, steady stream. The consistency should be that of mayonnaise. Set aside. When the soup is cooked, remove the bundle of herbs. Put the contents of soup pan into the food processor and work to a smooth purée. Strain, correct seasoning, and add some tomato paste for color, if necessary. Return soup to saucepan. Mix butter and flour into a paste. Add about 1 tsp of the paste to the soup, beating it in well, and bring the soup up to the boil. Add more paste as necessary to bring the soup to the consistency of thick cream. Stir in the cream. Serve the soup accompanied with the rouille, cheese and croûtons.

SERVES 4

Matelote

Akin to a chowder, this seafood soup is almost a meal in itself.

PREPARATION TIME: 20 minutes
COOKING TIME: 20 minutes

1lb sole
1lb monkfish
1 small wing of skate
8oz unpeeled shrimp
1 quart mussels
3 onions
6 tbsps butter

1⅔ cups dry cider or white wine
2 tbsps flour
2 tbsps chopped parsley
Salt
Freshly ground black pepper
Lemon juice

Fillet and skin the sole. Cut fillets into large pieces. Prepare monkfish in the same way. Chop wing of skate into 4 large pieces. Peel shrimp and set aside. Scrub mussels well, discarding any with broken shells. Chop the onion finely and soften in half the butter. Add mussels and about 3-4 tbsps water. Cover the pan and shake over a high heat until all mussels have opened, discarding any that have not. Strain liquid into a bowl, allow mussels to cool, then shell them. Put cooking liquid back into pan. Add wine or cider, and the pieces of fish so that they are barely covered by the liquid. Simmer gently for about 8 minutes or until fish is just cooked. Mix flour to a paste with the remaining butter. Remove cooked fish from liquid and put into a serving dish to keep warm. Bring liquid back to boil. Add the flour and butter paste, a little at a time, whisking it in and allowing liquid to boil after each addition, until liquid is thickened. Add the parsley, shelled prawns, shelled mussels, a little lemon juice, and seasoning. Heat for a few minutes to warm shellfish through. Pour this over the fish in the serving dish and sprinkle with more chopped parsley if desired.

This colorful stained-glass window is not in a church but in one of Paris' most
famous department stores, Au Printemps.

SERVES 6

Fennel Ramekins

These light fennel molds are easy to prepare and cook and, with their aniseed flavor, provide an original side dish or unusual appetizer.

PREPARATION TIME: 10 minutes
COOKING TIME: 1 hour

2lbs fennel bulb, cut into quarters
4 cups milk
4 eggs, beaten
1 tbsp Pernod, or other aniseed
   alcohol

¾ cup heavy cream
Salt and pepper
A little butter for greasing

Cut off any hard patches from the fennel and discard them. Cook the fennel in the milk for about 30 minutes, then leave to drain well. Once the fennel is well drained, put the quarters into a blender and blend until smooth – this should give about 2 cups of pulp. If necessary, make up to the desired amount by adding some of the cooking milk. Whisk in the eggs, aniseed, cream, salt and pepper.

Butter 6 ramekins and fill ¾ full with the fennel mixture. Place the ramekins in a high-sided, ovenproof dish, add water to come halfway up the sides of the ramekins, and cook in a warm oven for 30-40 minutes.

To serve, turn the flans out of the ramekins onto a preheated serving plate.

The château of Chenonceau is one of the most beautiful in the Loire Valley.
Presented by Henri II to his mistress, Diane de Poitiers, it was confiscated by
his wife, Catherine de Medicis, when Henri died.

SERVES 4

Tomates à la Languedocienne

This dish from the Languedoc region of southern France is similar to Provençal tomatoes, but is not as strong in flavor.

PREPARATION TIME: 15 minutes plus 1-2 hours for the tomatoes to drain.
COOKING TIME: 5-8 minutes

---

4 large ripe tomatoes
2 slices white bread, crusts
  removed
1 clove garlic, crushed

2 tbsps olive oil
1 tbsp chopped parsley
2 tsp chopped thyme or marjoram
Salt and pepper

Cut the tomatoes in half and score the cut surface. Sprinkle with salt and leave upside-down in a colander to drain. Allow the tomatoes to drain for 1-2 hours. Rinse the tomatoes and scoop out most of the juice and pulp.

    Mix the olive oil and garlic together and brush both sides of the bread with the mixture, leaving it to soften. Chop the herbs and the bread together until well mixed. Press the filling into the tomatoes and sprinkle with any remaining garlic and olive oil mixture. Cook the tomatoes in an ovenproof dish under a preheated broiler under low heat for the first 5 minutes. Then raise the dish or the heat to brown the tomatoes on top. Serve immediately.

A street artist paints numerous views of the harbor at St Tropez to sell to the many souvenir hunters in search of unusual mementos.

SERVES 4

Marjoram Potatoes and Onions

New ways with potatoes are always welcome and this adaptable dish can be cooked over a barbecue, which makes it doubly welcome.

PREPARATION TIME: 15 minutes
COOKING TIME: 40 minutes

---

4 medium-sized potatoes, peeled
  and sliced thickly
4 medium-sized onions, sliced
2 tsps marjoram, chopped

Salt and pepper
Butter

Layer the potatoes and onions in an ovenproof dish or in a piece of aluminum foil if barbecueing. Sprinkle with the marjoram, salt and pepper and dot with butter. Bake in a moderate oven, 350°F, for 40 minutes. Alternatively, cook over hot coals on a barbecue for 30-40 minutes.

Recipe courtesy Schwartz Spices Limited

Built between 1163 and 1330 in early Gothic style, the Cathedral of Notre-Dame is one of the most memorable sights in Paris.

SERVES 4

Lima Beans Provençale

To enjoy this tasty side dish at its best, use young fresh beans and fresh herbs.

PREPARATION TIME: 5 minutes
COOKING TIME: 8 minutes

1lb fresh or frozen lima beans
2 tbsps butter
2 tsps mixed herbs

4 tomatoes, peeled, seeded and diced
Salt and pepper

Cook the lima beans in boiling salted water until tender, about 8 minutes. Drain and refresh under cold water. Peel off outer skin if desired. Melt butter and toss with the broad beans and mixed herbs. Heat through and add the tomatoes, salt and pepper. Serve immediately.

The dressed stone of Château le Theil in Normandy. The area is justly famous for its historic buildings and fine cities, but is perhaps best known for the part it played in the Second World War as the arena for the D-Day landings and the Battle of Normandy.

SERVES 4

Artichauts Aioli

Home-made mayonnaise is in a class by itself. With the addition of garlic,
it makes a perfect sauce for artichokes – a typically Provençal appetizer.

PREPARATION TIME: 30 minutes
COOKING TIME: 25 minutes

---

4 medium-sized globe artichokes
1 slice lemon
1 bay leaf
Pinch salt

SAUCE AIOLI
2 egg yolks

2 cloves garlic, peeled and minced
1 cup olive oil
Salt, pepper and lemon juice to
    taste
Chervil, to garnish

To prepare the artichokes, break off the stems and twist to remove any tough fibers.
Trim the base so that the artichokes will stand upright. Trim the points from all the
leaves and wash the artichokes well. Bring a large saucepan or stockpot full of water to
the boil with the slice of lemon and the bay leaf. Add a pinch of salt and, when the
water is boiling, add the artichokes. Allow to cook for 25 minutes over a moderate
heat. While the artichokes are cooking, prepare the sauce.

Whisk the egg yolks and garlic with a pinch of salt and pepper in a deep bowl or in
a liquidizer or food processor. Add the olive oil a few drops at a time while whisking by
hand, or in a thin steady stream with the machine running. If preparing the sauce by
hand, once half the oil is added, the remainder may be added in a thin, steady stream.
Add lemon juice once the sauce becomes very thick. When all the oil has been added,
adjust the seasoning and add more lemon juice to taste.

When the artichokes are cooked, the bottom leaves will pull away easily. Remove
them from the water with a draining spoon and drain upside-down on paper towels or
in a colander. Allow to cool and serve with the sauce aioli. Garnish with chervil.

Two fourteenth-century towers dominate the harbor of the pretty port of La
Rochelle, on the Atlantic coast.

SERVES 4-6

Salade Bresse

This is an extremely sophisticated salad, equally suitable as a first course,
or as an accompaniment to a formal summer dinner.

PREPARATION TIME: 20 minutes

---

1 head Belgian endive, separated
  and washed
1 head cos lettuce, washed
1 bunch lamb's lettuce, or
  watercress, washed
4oz cherry tomatoes, halved and
  cored
4 chicken breasts, cooked, skinned
  and thinly sliced
4oz Bresse bleu, or other blue
  cheese, cut into small pieces

16 small pickles, thinly sliced
½ cup walnut halves
2 tbsps each vegetable and walnut
  oil, mixed
2 tsps white wine vinegar
¾ cup fromage frais
2 tsps chopped fresh tarragon
  leaves
Salt and pepper

Tear the Belgian endive and cos lettuce leaves into bite-sized pieces. Pull apart the
lamb's lettuce, but leave the leaves whole. If using watercress, remove any thick stems
and yellow leaves. Toss the lettuces together in a large salad bowl. Put the tomatoes,
chicken, cheese, pickles and walnuts on top of the lettuce and mix lightly. Put the oils
and vinegar together in a small bowl and whisk well, until they are thick. Fold in the
fromage frais and the tarragon leaves. Whisk well, then season to taste.

    Drizzle some of the dressing over the salad before serving. Put the rest of the dressing
into a small jug and hand it round separately.

Perfect vine-growing countryside at Château de la Saule, Massigny. A visit to
the vineyard to sample the local wines is an absolute must on any visit to
France.

SERVES 6

Pommes Dauphiné

The food from the mountainous province of Dauphiné is robust fare.
Comté is the finest cheese of the area and like Gruyère it is creamy rather
than stringy when melted.

PREPARATION TIME: 25 minutes
COOKING TIME: 30-40 minutes

1 clove garlic, peeled and crushed
   with the flat of a knife
2 tbsps butter
2¼lbs potatoes, peeled and thinly
   sliced
½ cup light cream

Salt and pepper
1½ cups grated Comté or Gruyère
   cheese
⅓ cup butter cut into very small
   dice

Preheat the oven to 400°F. Rub the bottom and sides of a heavy baking dish with the crushed clove of garlic. Grease the bottom and sides liberally with the butter. Use a dish that can also be employed as a serving dish. Spread half of the potato slices in the bottom of the dish, sprinkle with cheese, salt and pepper and dot with the butter dice. Top with the remaining slices of potato, neatly arranged. Sprinkle with the remaining cheese, salt, pepper and butter. Pour the cream into the side of the dish around the potatoes.

    Cook in the top part of the oven for 30-40 minutes, or until the potatoes are tender and the top is nicely browned. Serve immediately.

The picturesque town of Crest in the Drôme region is watched over by its
twelfth-century keep.

SERVES 6-8

Ratatouille

This is probably one of the most familiar dishes from southern France.
Either hot or cold, it's full of the warm sun of Provence.

PREPARATION TIME: 40 minutes
COOKING TIME: 35 minutes

---

2 eggplants, sliced and scored on
    both sides
4-6 zucchini, depending on size
3-6 tbsps olive oil
2 onions, peeled and thinly sliced
2 green peppers, seeded and cut
    into 1-inch pieces

1 large clove garlic, minced
2lbs ripe tomatoes, peeled and
    quartered
2 tsps chopped fresh basil or 1 tsp
    dried basil
Salt and pepper
½ cup dry white wine

Lightly salt the eggplant slices and place on paper towels to drain for about 30
minutes. Rinse and pat dry. Slice the zucchini thickly and set them aside.

    Pour 3 tbsps of the olive oil into a large frying pan and when hot, lightly brown the
onions, green peppers and zucchini slices. Remove the vegetables to a casserole and
add the eggplant slices to the frying pan or saucepan. Cook to brown both sides lightly
and place in the casserole with the other vegetables. Add extra oil as needed while
frying the vegetables.

    Add the garlic and tomatoes to the oil and cook for 1 minute. Add the garlic and
tomatoes to the rest of the vegetables along with any remaining olive oil in the frying
pan. Add basil, salt, pepper and wine and bring to the boil over moderate heat. Cover
and reduce to simmering. If the vegetables need moisture during cooking, add a little
white wine.

    When the vegetables are tender, remove them from the casserole to a serving dish
and rapidly boil any remaining liquid in the pan to reduce to about 2 tbsps. Pour over
the ratatouille to serve.

Notre-Dame at dusk – the cathedral has pride of place on an island in the middle
of the River Seine, from whose banks its awe-inspiring beauty is clearly visible.

SERVES 6

Herby Vegetables

Vegetables are often served as a separate course in France, and this dish is
certainly worthy of such treatment.

PREPARATION TIME: 25 minutes
COOKING TIME: 5 minutes

---

4 sticks celery	Pinch salt and pepper
4 medium zucchini	1 tsp chopped fresh oregano or
2 red peppers, seeded	marjoram
3-4 tbsps oil	4 tbsps snipped fresh chives

Slice the celery on the diagonal into pieces about 1½-inch thick. Cut the zucchini in
half lengthwise and then cut into ½-inch thick slices. Remove all the seeds and the
white pith from the peppers and cut them into diagonal pieces about 1 inch.

Heat the oil in a heavy frying pan over medium high heat. Add the celery and stir-
fry until barely tender. Add zucchini and peppers and stir-fry until all the vegetables
are tender crisp. Add the salt, pepper and oregano or marjoram and cook for 30
seconds more. Stir in the chives and serve immediately.

The cupolas, dome, and bell tower of the basilica of the Sacré Coeur in Paris.
Standing 336 feet high, it is a wonderful vantage point from which to view the
city.

SERVES 4-6

Haricots Verts à l'Oignon

These slender green beans are the classic French vegetable. Quickly
blanched, then refreshed under cold water, they can be reheated and still
stay beautifully green.

PREPARATION TIME: 15 minutes
COOKING TIME: 8-10 minutes

1lb green beans	1 medium-sized onion
1oz butter	Salt and pepper

Top and tail the beans. Cook the beans whole in boiling salted water for about 8-10
minutes. Meanwhile, finely chop the onion.

Melt the butter and fry the finely chopped onion until lighly brown. Drain the
beans and toss them over heat to dry. Pour the butter and onions over the beans and
season with salt and pepper. Serve immediately.

The deep bay at Villefranche-sur-Mer provides good anchorage for large ships
as well as for the smaller, local fishing craft. The little fishermen's chapel of St-
Pierre, with its biblical scenes painted by Jean Cocteau,
is one of the town's most famous attractions

SERVES 6
Broccoli Gratin

A typically French way of serving tasty broccoli.

PREPARATION TIME: 10 minutes
COOKING TIME: 55 minutes

---

3 large heads broccoli, waste and
   hard stalks removed
2 tbsps butter
¼ cup flour
1 cup milk

4 tbsps heavy cream
Pinch nutmeg
Salt and pepper
¾ cup shredded cheese

Cook the broccoli heads in salted boiling water until just underdone and slightly crisp. Plunge them immediately into cold water to stop them from cooking any further, and drain well.

Make the white sauce by melting the butter in a saucepan, stirring in the flour, cooking for one minute and then beating in all the milk in one go. Beat continuously for 2 minutes. Remove the sauce from the heat, and stir in the cream, nutmeg, salt, pepper and half of the cheese.

Chop the broccoli roughly with a sharp knife, mix into the sauce and pour into an ovenproof dish. Sprinkle over the remaining cheese and cook in a hot oven, 400°F, for approximately 15 minutes, until the top is crisp and brown.

The mysterious ruined village of Les Baux in Provence has a strange history – it
was once the home of a madman who was said to throw his dinner guests to
their deaths from the clifftop.

SERVES 6

Petits pois à la Française

Fresh peas cooked with onions and carrots make a colorful vegetable
combination to accompany a wide variety of dishes.

PREPARATION TIME: 25 minutes
COOKING TIME: 20 minutes

2¼lbs fresh peas (about 7lbs in the
   pod)
¼ cup butter
1 lettuce, finely shredded
6 onions, finely chopped

2 tsps sugar
1 bouquet garni
Salt and pepper
2 carrots, peeled and finely diced

Rinse the peas under cold water and leave to drain.
   In a heavy-based saucepan, melt the butter and gently cook the peas, lettuce, onion,
sugar, bouquet garni, salt and pepper for 5 minutes. Increase the heat, add 1 inch water,
bring to the boil and add the carrots. Cover the saucepan, reduce the heat to very low
and cook for 15-20 minutes, or until the peas are cooked through. Remove the bouquet
garni and serve.

Night falls over Paris, and the Eiffel Tower is silhouetted against the soft glow
of the setting sun.

SERVES 4

Glazed Carrots

Carrots cooked in this unbelievably simple and delicious way are
extremely good with lamb dishes.

PREPARATION TIME: 15 minutes
COOKING TIME: 15-20 minutes

¼ cup butter
1lb young carrots, scraped and
    quartered lengthwise
Salt and pepper
Pinch of sugar

GARNISH
Knob of butter
Chopped fresh parsley

Melt the butter in a pan. Add the carrots, seasoning, sugar and enough water to cover.
Cook slowly without a lid for about 15 minutes, until the carrots are soft and the water
has evaporated, leaving the carrots with a slight glaze. Serve in a warm dish. Garnish
with a knob of butter and chopped parsley.

The city of Avignon is dominated by the Palace of the Popes, built in the
fourteenth century when the papacy moved out of Rome, finding it too corrupt.

The beauty of the offshore mount of Mont St-Michel belies the care with which
it should be explored – it is surrounded by patches of quicksand and the tide
often comes in with alarming speed.

SERVES 4

Imperial Asparagus

Aspargus is always an impressive dish and is especially appropriate for special occasions

PREPARATION TIME: 30 minutes
COOKING TIME: 20-30 minutes

2lbs white asparagus
3 tbsps butter or margarine
3 tbsps flour
1 cup chicken stock or aparagus
   cooking liquid

½ cup French white wine
2 egg yolks
4 tbsps heavy cream
Salt and white pepper
Pinch sugar

Trim the ends of the asparagus to remove the top parts and to make the spears the same length. Using a swivel vegetable peeler, pare the stalks up to the tips.

To cook the asparagus, tie the spears in a bundle and stand them upright in a deep saucepan of lightly salted boiling water. Alternatively, place the spears in a large sauté pan of boiling salted water. If using a sauté pan, place half on and half off the heat, with the tips of the asparagus off the heat. Cook, uncovered, for about 12-15 minutes, or until the asparagus is tender. Drain and reserve the cooking liquid. Keep the asparagus warm in a covered serving dish.

To prepare the sauce, melt the butter in a heavy-based saucepan and stir in the flour off the heat. Gradually beat in the asparagus cooking liquid or chicken stock and add the wine. Stir until the sauce is smooth and then place over a low heat. Bring the sauce to the boil, stirring constantly, and allow to boil for about 1-2 minutes, or until thickened.

Beat the egg yolks and cream together and add a few spoonfuls of the hot sauce. Return the egg and cream mixture to the pan, stirring constantly. Reheat if necessary, but do not allow the sauce to boil once the egg is added. Add salt and white pepper and a pinch of sugar if desired. Pour over the asparagus to serve.

SERVES 4

Herby Goat Cheese

Fresh goat's cheese is very popular in France, and is becoming more popular in other parts of the world. Its sometimes bland flavor is enlivened by the addition of herbs in this recipe.

PREPARATION TIME: 40 minutes

2 fresh goat cheeses
1 tbsp mixed fresh herbs, such as
   chives, parsley and chervil
1 tbsp finely chopped onion and
   shallot
10 capers

5 peppercorns
Salt and pepper
Few drops vinegar
Few drops lemon juice
½ tsp olive oil

Mix the cheeses with the chopped herbs, onion and shallot. Mix in the capers, peppercorns and the salt and pepper. Stir in the vinegar, lemon juice and olive oil. Stir well. Place the cheese into 4 small custard cups, pushing it down well, and then set in the refrigerator for approximately 2 hours. Turn out just before serving.

The Arc de Triomphe in Paris was built in honor of Napoleon's victorious army, and is grand in its proportions – being 164 feet high and 148 feet wide.

MAKES 1 omelet

Omelette Roussillon

Roussillon is on France's border with Spain. The Spanish influence is evident in the use of tomatoes and peppers combined with eggs.

PREPARATION TIME: 15 minutes
COOKING TIME: 5 minutes

3 eggs
Salt and pepper
1 tbsp butter or margarine
¼ green pepper, cut into small
 dice

2 tomatoes, peeled, seeded and
 roughly chopped
2oz ham, cut into small dice

Break the eggs into a bowl, season with salt and pepper and beat to mix thoroughly. Heat an omelet pan and drop in the butter, swirling it so that it coats the bottom and sides. When the butter stops foaming, add pepper and ham. Cook for 1-2 minutes to soften slightly, and add the tomatoes. Pour in the eggs and, as they begin to cook, push the cooked portion with the flat of the fork to allow the uncooked portion underneath. Continue to lift the eggs and shake the pan to prevent them from sticking.

When the egg on top is still slightly creamy, fold ⅓ of the omelet to the center and tip it out of the pan onto a warm serving dish, folded side down. Serve immediately.

Martiques, in the Provence region of France. The area is steeped in history, with much evidence of the Romans in particular remaining. Their influence is also obvious in the distinctly Romanesque architecture of many of the churches.

SERVES 6

Quiche Lorraine

This classic flan from northeastern France has a pedigree stretching back several hundred years.

PREPARATION TIME: 30 minutes
COOKING TIME: 45 minutes

DOUGH
1 cup flour
Pinch of salt
⅓ cup butter or margarine
1 tbsp lard
Cold water

FILLING
1 tbsp butter or margarine

4 strips bacon
10 green onions, cut into 2-inch
    slices
2 eggs, beaten
¼ cup Gruyère cheese, shredded
⅔ cup light cream
½ tsp dried mustard
Salt
Pepper

Sift flour and salt into a bowl. Cut cold fats into small pieces and drop into flour. Cut fats into flour. When well cut in, use fingers to rub in completely. Mix to a firm but pliable dough with cold water. Knead on a lightly floured board until smooth. Chill for 15 minutes in the refrigerator. Roll out on a lightly floured board and use to line a 9-inch flan ring.

Melt the butter in a frying pan and add the bacon and green onions, fry gently until they turn a light golden-brown color. Place in a bowl. Add the beaten eggs, cheese, cream, mustard and salt and pepper to taste, and stir well. Pour into prepared pastry shell. Bake in preheated oven, 370°F, for 20-25 minutes until golden brown. Serve hot or cold.

A dramatic sunset over Cannes. The town was once just a small fishing port
until wealthy aristocrats adopted it as the perfect summer resort.

SERVES 4

Omelette aux Fruits de Mer

This dish makes a lovely summer lunch, if served with a salad and new potatoes.

PREPARATION TIME: 5 minutes
COOKING TIME: 7-10 minutes

½ pint shelled mussels
½ pint shelled clams
6-8 eggs
Drop of anchovy paste
Cayenne pepper

Salt
Pepper
2½ tbsps butter
Finely chopped parsley and chives

Poach the mussels in boiling salted water for about 2 minutes. Add a bay leaf if desired. Rinse the clams under cold water. Separate eggs and beat the yolks with the anchovy paste, cayenne pepper and seasoning. Whisk the egg whites until stiff but not dry and fold into the yolks. Heat the butter in a large omelet pan and when foaming pour in the egg mixture. Allow eggs to set on the bottom. Score the omelet down the middle. Add clams and mussels and fold the omelet in two. Heat through for 2 minutes to cook the inside of the omelet and to warm the shellfish. Serve immediately, sprinkled with finely chopped parsley and chives.

The Moulin Rouge in the Montmartre district of Paris. The area still retains some of the cosmopolitan air of the days when writers such as Ernest Hemingway and, later, Jean-Paul Sartre held court in the local cafés.

The Palace of Versailles was commissioned by King Louis XIV in 1661, and
work on the mammoth task continued for over fifty years. The original splendor
of the palace and its grounds has now been preserved for the benefit of the
whole nation – and for the thousands of tourists who flock to the palace every
year.

SERVES 4-6
Seafood Crêpes

Savory crêpes are as popular as sweet ones in France, and are often served as "fast food" from street stalls.

PREPARATION TIME: 45 minutes
COOKING TIME: 20 minutes

CRÊPE BATTER
1 cup flour
Pinch of salt
2 medium eggs
1 cup milk
1 tbsp olive oil or vegetable oil
Oil to grease pan

FILLING
4oz shrimp, peeled and deveined

2 scallops, cleaned and sliced
4oz whitefish fillets
Squeeze of lemon juice
4 tbsps butter or margarine
8 green onions, sliced
3 tbsps flour
1¼ cups milk
1 tbsp lemon juice
Salt
Pepper

Sift the flour and salt into a bowl. Make a well in the center and drop in the eggs. Start to mix in the eggs gradually, taking in flour around edges. When becoming stiff, add a little milk until all the flour has been incorporated. Beat to a smooth batter, then add remaining milk. Stir in the oil. Cover bowl and leave in a cool place for 30 minutes. Heat small frying pan or 7-inch crêpe pan. Wipe over with oil. When hot, add enough batter mixture to cover base of pan when rolled. Pour off any excess batter. When brown on underside, loosen and turn over with a spatula and brown on other side. Pile on a plate and cover with a clean towel until needed. Poach scallops and fish in water with a squeeze of lemon juice for 4 minutes or until cooked through. Melt the butter in a pan. Add the green onions and cook for 3 minutes. Remove with slotted spoon and set aside. Stir in the flour and cook for 1 minute. Remove from heat and gradually stir in milk. Return to heat, bring to the boil, and cook for 3 minutes, stirring continuously. Add green onions, seafood and lemon juice, and salt and pepper and stir well until heated through. Do not reboil. Divide the mixture evenly between the crêpes and roll up or fold into triangles. Place in a baking dish and cover with aluminum foil. Heat in a hot oven, 400°F, for 10 minutes. Serve immediately.

SERVES 4

Red Snapper Niçoise

This version of the classic Salade Niçoise incorporates red snapper for a
more substantial dish.

PREPARATION TIME: 15 minutes
COOKING TIME: 15 minutes

4 small, whole red snappers
1lb ripe tomatoes
2 hard-cooked eggs
½ cup pitted black olives
½ cup mushrooms
1 green pepper
Small can anchovy fillets
1 clove garlic, minced
1 chopped shallot
Seasoned flour

2 tbsps olive oil
Lemon juice
Salt
Pepper

VINAIGRETTE DRESSING
2 tbsps red wine vinegar
6 tbsps olive oil
¼ tsp Dijon mustard
Handful of chopped mixed herbs
  (eg. basil, oregano, thyme)

Scale and clean fish, trimming fins but leaving head and tail on. Cut tomatoes into
quarters and remove cores. Cut eggs into quarters. Cut olives in half, lengthwise. If
mushrooms are small, leave whole; if not, quarter them. Cut green pepper into thin
slices, and cut anchovies in half, lengthwise. Prepare vinaigrette dressing and add
chopped herbs, garlic and shallot. Put in the mushrooms and leave to marinate in the
refrigerator for about 1 hour. Meanwhile, toss fish in seasoned flour to coat lightly. Heat
2 tbsps olive oil in a frying pan and fry fish on both sides until cooked through – about
2-3 minutes per side. When cooking the second side, sprinkle over some lemon juice.
Season lightly, and leave to go cold. When ready to serve, add tomatoes, green
peppers, eggs and olives to the mushrooms in their marinade, and toss. Pile the salad
into a serving dish and arrange the cold, cooked red snapper on top. Garnish with
anchovy strips.

Pommard in the Champagne region of France is situated in classic vine-growing
country.

SERVES 4

Skate with Capers, Olives and Shallots

Restaurants throughout France offer this mouthwatering dish as part of their repertoire, yet it's simple enough to serve at home for a weekday supper.

PREPARATION TIME: 10 minutes
COOKING TIME: 15 minutes

---

4 wings of skate	½ cup butter
1¼ cups dry white wine and water mixed	2 shallots, chopped
	2 tbsps capers
1 bay leaf	½ cup pitted black olives, sliced
Salt	1 tbsp chopped mixed herbs
4 peppercorns	Lemon juice

Put the skate into a baking pan with the wine, water, bay leaf, salt and peppercorns. Cover and poach in a moderate oven, 350°F, for 10 minutes. Drain well, removing any skin, and keep warm. Melt the butter and cook the shallots quickly, to brown both. Add capers and olives to heat through. Add herbs and lemon juice. Pour over the skate and serve immediately.

The Place de la Concorde is arguably one of the most beautiful squares in the world. Built for Louis XV, it was, ironically, the place where Louis XVI, and his queen Marie Antoinette, were beheaded.

SERVES 4

Scallops in Saffron Sauce

This unusual dish is redolent of the Mediterranean.

PREPARATION TIME: 15 minutes
COOKING TIME: 15 minutes

---

16 large scallops with coral
    attached
½ cup water
½ cup dry white wine
1 shallot, roughly chopped
1 bouquet garni, consisting of 1 bay
    leaf, 1 sprig of fresh thyme and 3
    stalks of parsley

6 black peppercorns
A few strands of saffron
4 tbsps hot water
1¼ cups heavy cream
3 tbsps fresh chopped parsley
Salt and pepper

Put the scallops into a large shallow pan together with the water, wine, shallot, bouquet garni and peppercorns. Cover the pan and bring the liquid almost to the boil. Remove the pan from the heat and leave the scallops to poach in the hot liquid for 10-15 minutes. The scallops are cooked when they are just firm to the touch. Remove them from the liquid and keep warm on a clean plate. Strain the scallop cooking liquid into a small saucepan and bring to the boil. Allow the liquid to boil rapidly until it is reduced by about half.

Soak the saffron in the hot water for about 5 minutes, or until the color has infused into the water. Add the saffron with its soaking liquid, the heavy cream and the chopped parsley to the reduced cooking liquid and season to taste. Bring the sauce back to just below boiling point.

Arrange the scallops on a serving plate and pour a little of the sauce over them before serving.

The River Orb at Béziers. The town lies near the coast and its restaurants
provide deliciously fresh fish and seafood dishes all year round.

SERVES 4

Monkfish Piperade

Turn the classic piperade into a more filling dish by adding monkfish and
serving with French bread croûtons.

PREPARATION TIME: 20 minutes
COOKING TIME: 30 minutes

---

2 onions
2-3 tbsps olive oil
1 yellow pepper
1 red pepper
1 green pepper
1-2 cloves garlic

1 small can tomatoes
Salt
Pepper
1½lbs monkfish fillets
1 small loaf of French bread
Oil for deep-frying

Slice the onions thinly and soften in 1 tbsp olive oil in a saucepan. Slice all the
peppers in half, remove seeds, and cut into ½-inch strips. Mince the garlic and add to
the onions when tender, then cook gently for another 5 minutes. Add the tomatoes
and seasoning and let the sauce simmer until liquid has reduced by about half. If the
fish fillets are large, cut them in half again lengthwise. Heat the remaining oil in a
saucepan and cook the fish until it is lightly brown. Transfer fish to an overproof dish,
and when the piperade is ready, spoon it over the top of the fillets, and heat through in
a moderate oven, 350°F, for about 10 minutes. Meanwhile, slice the French bread on
the slant into ½-inch slices. Fry in enough oil to barely cover until golden brown, then
drain on paper towels. Put the monkfish piperade into a serving dish and surround
with the French bread croûtons.

Nice (facing page) is undoubtedly the capital of the Riviera and its main
promenade is lined with fabulous hotels which overlook the waters of the
Mediterranean.

SERVES 6

Fruits de mer en Casserole

This makes the most of the delicious and varied fish and shellfish found off France's Mediterranean coast.

PREPARATION TIME: 35 minutes
COOKING TIME: 20 minutes

---

24 clams or mussels in the shell
3 squid
2lb firm whitefish, filleted into
    2-inch pieces
3 medium-sized tomatoes, peeled,
    seeded and chopped

½ green pepper, seeded and
    chopped
1 small onion, chopped
1 clove garlic, finely chopped
1 cup dry white wine
Salt and pepper
½ cup olive oil
6 slices French bread
3 tbsps chopped parsley

Scrub the clams or mussels well to remove the beards and barnacles. Discard any shellfish with broken shells or ones that do not close when tapped. Place the mussels or clams in a large saucepan or heatproof casserole, scatter over about half of the vegetables and garlic and spoon over 4 tbsps of the olive oil.

To clean the squid, hold the tail section in one hand and the head section in the other to pull the tail away from the head. Cut the tentacles free from the head just above the eyes. Discard the head, entrails and ink sack. Remove the quill from the body of the squid and peel away the reddish-purple outer skin. Slice the tail into strips about ½-inch thick. Cut the tentacles into individual pieces.

Scatter the squid and the prepared whitefish over the vegetables in the pan and top with the remaining vegetables. Pour over the white wine and season with salt and pepper. Bring to the boil over high heat and then reduce to simmering. Cover the pan and cook for about 20 minutes or until the clams open, the squid is tender and the fish flakes easily. Discard any clams or mussels that do not open.

Heat the remaining olive oil in a frying pan and when hot, add the slices of bread, browning them well on both sides. Drain on paper towels. Place a slice of bread in the bottom of a soup bowl and ladle the fish mixture over the bread. Sprinkle with parsley and serve immediately.

The gentle waters of the Loire River amble through the ancient town of Amboise, where they are crossed by a modern bridge but overlooked by a historic château.

SERVES 4

Mussels in Lemon Cream

Mussels are a great French favorite and are beautifully complemented in
this recipe by a tangy lemon sauce.

PREPARATION TIME: 10 minutes
COOKING TIME: 10 minutes

1 quart mussels
Flour or oatmeal
2 tbsps butter
1 shallot, finely chopped

Grated rind and juice of 2 lemons
1¼ cups heavy cream
2 tbsps chopped parsley

Scrub the mussels well, discarding any with broken shells. Put into a bowl with clean,
cold water, and add a handful of flour or oatmeal. Leave for ½ hour, then drain and
rinse mussels under clean running water. Put the butter and finely chopped shallot into
a large pan and cook until shallot is soft, but not colored. Add lemon juice, then
mussels. Cover and cook quickly, shaking the pan until mussel shells open. Discard
any that do not open. Remove mussels and keep them warm. Strain the liquid and
return it to the rinsed-out pan. Add the cream and bring to the boil. Allow to boil for
5 minutes to thicken slightly. Pour over the mussels, and sprinkle with grated lemon
rind and chopped parsley.

An elevator ride to the top of the Arc de Triomphe affords the tourist a
marvelous view of "The Star" – the twelve avenues which converge at the arch.

SERVES 4

Quenelles au Beurre Blanc

These quenelles, in their rich, buttery sauce, make a sophisticated
appetizer, best followed by something simple, such as Steak au Poivre.

PREPARATION TIME: 25 minutes
COOKING TIME: 20 minutes

1lb pike or other whitefish
2 cups white breadcrumbs
4 tbsps milk
6 tbsps butter
2 eggs
Salt
Pepper
Nutmeg
Cayenne pepper

BEURRE BLANC SAUCE
1 small onion, peeled and chopped
   finely
1 tbsp white wine vinegar

3 tbsps dry white wine
½ cup unsalted butter
2 tbsps lemon juice
1 tsp snipped chives
Salt

VEGETABLE GARNISH
1 carrot, peeled
1 stick celery, washed and trimmed
1 medium-sized zucchini, topped
   and tailed
1 leek, trimmed, with some green
   attached

First prepare quenelle mixture. Skin and bone fish and cut into small pieces. Place in a
food processor bowl. Soak the breadcrumbs in milk; drain away most of the liquid, and
put into the food processor with the fish. Melt the butter and pour into the fish
mixture with the machine running. Work mixture to a smooth purée. Add the eggs,
continuing to mix until smooth. Add salt and pepper, cayenne pepper and nutmeg.
Chill mixture in refrigerator for at least 1 hour, or overnight.

To cook quenelles, fill a sauté pan with salted water. Bring to the boil. Reduce heat
until water is just simmering. With two spoons, shape quenelles into little ovals. Poach
them in water for about 6 minutes, turning them over about halfway through. Remove
them with a slotted spoon. Drain and put them in a dish to keep warm in the oven,
covered. To prepare beurre blanc sauce, put chopped onion into a small saucepan with
the vinegar and wine. Bring to boil and allow to reduce by half. Remove pan from
heat, and allow to cool a little. Cut butter into small pieces and add to onion mixture,
a little at a time, whisking well to a creamy sauce. After 2-3 pieces have been added,
place pan back over low heat and continue whisking until all butter has been added.
Season the sauce, add lemon juice, and strain. Add the snipped chives and serve hot
over the quenelles.

To prepare the garnish, cut all vegetables into 2-inch lengths, then cut those into
thin strips. Bring water to the boil in a large saucepan, with a pinch of salt. Cook
carrots for about 5 minutes. Then add celery strips and cook for another 5 minutes.
Add zucchini and leek, and cook for 3 minutes more. Drain vegetables well, add them
to the sauce and pour over the quenelles to serve.

The remains of Napoleon lie in the crypt of the Eglise du Dôme, itself part of
the Hôtel des Invalides, in Paris. The tomb of France's greatest soldier contains
six coffins – the remains of the emperor being deposited in the innermost.

SERVES 4

Goujons

Tartare sauce is the authentic one to serve with this dish, but two
alternatives are given here, which are equally delicious.

PREPARATION TIME: 20-30 minutes
COOKING TIME: 2-3 minutes

---

2 sole
Seasoned flour
1 egg
2 tsps olive oil
Dry breadcrumbs
Oil for deep-frying
Pinch of salt

TARTARE SAUCE
2 tbsps mayonnaise
1 tbsp heavy cream
2 tsps chopped parsley
2 tsps chopped dill pickles
2 tsps chopped capers
1 tsp chopped onion

CURRY SAUCE
2 tbsps mayonnaise
1 tbsp heavy cream
1 tsp curry powder
1½ tsps mango relish

TOMATO HERB SAUCE
2 tbsps mayonnaise
1 tbsp heavy cream
1 tsp chopped parsley
1 tsp chopped tarragon
1 tsp chopped chives
1 tsp tomato paste
Squeeze of lemon

Fillet the sole and skin the fillets. Rinse fillets in cold water and pat dry. Cut each fillet
on the diagonal into pieces about ½-inch thick and 2½-3 inches long. Coat
thoroughly with seasoned flour, shaking off any excess. Beat the eggs lightly and mix in
the olive oil. Dip fish pieces into the mixture and roll them in the breadcrumbs. Put
fish aside in a cool place: do not coat the fish too soon before cooking. Mix ingredients
for the various sauces and set aside. Heat oil in a deep-fat fryer to about 375°F. Put fish
in the frying basket and lower into the hot oil. Fry for 2-3 minutes until crisp and
golden brown. Fry in small batches. Drain fish on crumpled paper towels, sprinkle
lightly with salt, and then pile the fish into a hot serving dish. Garnish with wedges of
lemon and sprigs of parsley, if desired, and serve the sauces separately for dipping the
fish.

SERVES 4
Moules Marinière

Brittany and Normandy are famous for mussels and for cream and so cooks combined the two in one perfect seafood dish.

PREPARATION TIME: 30 minutes
COOKING TIME: 15 minutes

3lbs mussels
1½ cups dry cider or white wine
4 shallots, finely chopped
1 clove garlic, crushed

1 bouquet garni
½ cup heavy cream
3 tbsps butter, cut into small pieces
2 tbsps finely chopped parsley

Scrub the mussels well and remove the beards and any barnacles from the shells. Discard any mussels that have cracked shells and do not open when lightly tapped. Put the mussels into a large bowl and soak in cold water for at least 1 hour. Meanwhile, chop the parsley very finely.

Bring the cider or wine to the boil in a large stock pot and add the shallots, garlic and bouquet garni. Add the mussels, cover the pan and cook for 5 minutes. Shake the pan or stir the mussels around frequently until the shells open. Lift out the mussels into a large soup tureen or individual serving bowls. Discard any mussels that have not opened.

Reduce the cooking liquid by about half and strain into another saucepan. Add the cream and bring to the boil to thicken slightly. Beat in the butter, a few pieces at a time. Adjust the seasoning, add the parsley and pour the sauce over the mussels to serve.

Rows and rows of grapevines line a hillside near the wine village of Vouvray in the Loire Valley.

SERVES 6

Poulet au Riz

This classic chicken dish from Alsace is served on a bed of rice with a rich, creamy sauce.

PREPARATION TIME: 15 minutes
COOKING TIME: 1 hour

---

1 large stewing chicken, cleaned
   and dried
Juice of 1 lemon
1 onion, chopped
1 carrot, chopped
1 leek, chopped
1 stick celery, finely chopped

1 bouquet garni
¼ cup butter
½ cup flour
1 cup heavy cream
Salt and pepper
6 portions of cooked long grain
   rice

Put the chicken in a large saucepan and cover with cold water. Bring to the boil and as soon as the water is boiling well, remove the bird and drain well. Separate the wings, thighs and the breasts. Sprinkle the lemon juice over the pieces of meat. Break up the carcass.

Put the carcass bones back into the saucepan, cover with water, and add all the vegetables, the bouquet garni and the pieces of meat. Bring to the boil, cover, reduce the heat and simmer until the meat is tender. Remove the pieces of meat and keep them warm. Boil what remains in the saucepan and allow it to reduce. Skim off any fat that rises to the top. Strain the sauce through a fine sieve and discard everything but the strained liquid.

In another saucepan, melt the butter and stir in the flour. Stir in the strained juices and continue stirring until the sauce thickens. Cook for a few minutes more and then stir in the cream and add salt and pepper. Serve the pieces of chicken on a bed of rice with the sauce poured over.

Facing page: sunset over the River Seine in Paris. At night the city is as lively as during the day with both tourists and Parisians crowding its numerous cafés and restaurants.

SERVES 4

Poulet Sauté Vallée d'Auge

This dish contains all the ingredients that Normandy is famous for – butter, cream, apples and Calvados.

PREPARATION TIME: 25-30 minutes
COOKING TIME: 55-60 minutes

¼ cup butter or margarine
2 tbsps oil
1 3lb chicken, cut into eight pieces
4 tbsps Calvados
⅓ cup chicken stock
2 apples, peeled, cored and
    coarsely chopped
2 sticks celery, finely chopped
1 shallot, finely chopped
½ tsp dried thyme, crumbled

⅓ cup heavy cream
2 egg yolks, lightly beaten
Salt and white pepper

GARNISH
1 bunch watercress or small parsley
    sprigs
2 apples, quartered, cored and cut
    into cubes
2 tbsps butter
Sugar

Melt half the butter and all of the oil in a large sauté pan over moderate heat. When the foam begins to subside, brown the chicken, a few pieces at a time, skin side down first. When all the chicken is browned, pour off most of the fat from the pan and return the chicken to the pan.

Pour the Calvados into a ladle or small saucepan and warm over gentle heat. Ignite with a match and pour, while still flaming, over the chicken. Shake the sauté pan gently until the flames subside. If the Calvados should flare up, cover the pan immediately with the lid.

Pour over the stock and scrape any browned chicken juices from the bottom of the pan. Set the chicken aside. Melt the remaining butter in a small saucepan or frying pan. Cook the chopped apples, shallot and celery and the thyme for about 10 minutes or until soft but not brown. Spoon over the chicken and return the pan to the high heat. Bring to the boil, then reduce heat, cover the pan and simmer 50 minutes. When the chicken is cooked, beat the eggs and cream. With a whisk, gradually beat in some of the hot sauce. Pour the mixture back into a saucepan and cook over a low heat for 2-3 minutes, stirring constantly until the sauce thickens and coats the back of a spoon. Season the sauce with salt and white pepper and set aside while preparing the garnish.

Put the remaining butter in a small frying pan and when foaming, add the apple. Toss over a high heat until beginning to soften. Sprinkle with sugar and cook until the apple begins to caramelize. To serve, coat the chicken with the sauce and decorate with watercress or parsley. Spoon the caramelized apples over the chicken.

The spectacular view from the Place de la Concorde toward the Eiffel Tower.

SERVES 4

Poulet Grillé au Limon

Crisp chicken with a tang of limes makes an elegant yet quickly-made entrée. From the warm regions of southern France, it is perfect for a summer meal.

PREPARATION TIME: 25 minutes, plus 4 hours marinating time
COOKING TIME: 35 minutes

2 2lb chickens	4 limes
1 tsp basil	Salt, pepper and sugar
⅓ cup olive oil	

Remove the leg ends, neck and wing tips from the chicken and discard them. Split the chicken in half, cutting away the backbone completely and discarding it. Loosen the ball and socket joint in the leg and flatten each half of the chicken by hitting it with the flat side of a cleaver.

Season the chicken on both sides with salt and pepper and sprinkle over the basil. Place the chicken in a shallow dish and pour over 2 tbsps of the olive oil. Squeeze the juice from 2 of the limes over the chicken. Cover and leave to marinate in the refrigerator for 4 hours.

Heat the broiler to its highest setting and preheat the oven to 375°F. Remove the chicken from the marinade and place in the broiler pan. Cook one side until golden brown and turn the pieces over. Sprinkle with 1 tbsp olive oil and brown the other side.

Place the chicken in a roasting dish, sprinkle with the remaining oil and roast in the oven for about 25 minutes. Peel the remaining limes and slice them thinly. When the chicken is cooked, place the lime slices on top and sprinkle lightly with sugar. Place under the broiler for a few minutes to caramelize the sugar and cook the limes. Place in a serving dish and spoon over any remaining marinade and the cooking juices. Serve immediately.

One of the three beautiful stained-glass rose windows in Notre-Dame Cathedral, Paris.

SERVES 4-6

Chicken Stew Niçoise

Nice, in southern France, has lent its name to many of the dishes that are
typical of French Mediterranean cookery.

PREPARATION TIME: 25 minutes
COOKING TIME: 40-60 minutes

---

4 tbsps olive oil
3lbs chicken, cut into 8 pieces
6 small onions or shallots, peeled
2 cloves garlic, minced
2lbs fresh tomatoes, peeled, seeded
   and chopped, or the same
   quantity of canned tomatoes,
   drained and broken up.

⅓ cup white wine
1 tsp chopped fresh marjoram
Bouquet garni (sprigs thyme, 1 bay
   leaf, 3 parsley stalks)
1 cup pitted black olives
Lemon juice
Salt and pepper

Heat half the oil in a large sauté pan or heatproof casserole. Add the chicken, skin side
down, in one layer. Cook over a moderate heat until golden brown on both sides,
turning once. Transfer the chicken to a plate and add the remaining oil to the pan if
necessary. Add the onions and cook, turning often to brown evenly. Add garlic and
cook for 1 minute. Add tomatoes, wine and marjoram. Tie the bouquet garni
ingredients with string and add to the pan along with the salt and pepper. Bring the
liquid to the boil and return the chicken to the pan. Cover and simmer for 20 minutes.
Uncover the pan and continue to simmer for another 15-20 minutes or until the
chicken is tender. Remove chicken breasts earlier if they cook before the rest of the
chicken. When all the chicken is cooked, remove it and the onions to a serving dish.
Remove the bouquet garni and add the olives to the sauce. Cook the sauce rapidly to
reduce it, stirring constantly, about 5 minutes. Add lemon juice if desired and pour
over the chicken to serve.

Marseille (above) is one of the most important ports in the Mediterranean and
for over 2,600 years its natural harbor has been the destination of numerous
trading ships.

Santenay epitomizes rural France for many people – a small, sleepy town
surrounded by acres of grapevines.

SERVES 6

Rabbit Casserole Normande

Normandy is famous for its apples and also for the cider and Calvados, or apple brandy, that are made from them. This recipe uses the former to good effect.

PREPARATION TIME: 30 minutes
COOKING TIME: 2 hours 20 minutes

---

1 3lb rabbit
¼ cup seasoned flour
¼ cup butter
½ cup shallots, chopped
2 carrots, sliced
2 parsnips, sliced
1 small tart apple, peeled, cored
   and chopped

2½ cups cider
1 tbsp made mustard
2 tsps casserole seasoning
½ tsp thyme
Seasoning
1 bay leaf

Preheat the oven to 350°F. Cut the rabbit into six serving pieces. Coat these with the seasoned flour. Melt the butter in a flameproof casserole. Add the rabbit and brown on all sides. Remove the rabbit from the pan, then add the shallots, carrots, parsnips and apple and fry until lightly colored. Pour in the cider, and stir in the mustard and casserole seasoning. Heat gently, stirring continuously, until just simmering, then return the rabbit pieces to the pan. Add the thyme and the bay leaf, cover the casserole and place it in the oven. Cook for 1½-2 hours, until the rabbit is tender. Taste and adjust the seasoning. Discard the bay leaf before serving.

SERVES 4

Coq au Vin

Red wine turns a chicken casserole from an everyday dish into something special enough for entertaining.

PREPARATION TIME: 15 minutes
COOKING TIME: 50-60 minutes

¼lb bacon, cut into cubes
2 tbsps butter
3lbs chicken pieces
12 small white onions, peeled and
    left whole
2 cups mushrooms, sliced
2 bay leaves
2 cloves garlic, minced
1 bouquet garni

3 cups full-bodied red wine
3 tbsps beurre manié (1 tbsp all-
    purpose flour blended with 2
    tbsps softened butter)
Salt and black pepper

GARNISH
Fried bread croûtons
Parsley

Fry the bacon until it has browned and rendered its fat and, with a slotted spoon, remove from the pan. Next add the butter to the fat and melt over a gentle heat. When the foam subsides, add the chicken joints and fry until golden on both sides. Remove them to a large flameproof casserole. Fry the onions until a little brown and then lightly fry the mushrooms.

Add the onions and mushrooms to the casserole together with the bacon, garlic, bay leaves and bouquet garni. Pour over the red wine and season with black pepper and a little salt. Bring to a steady simmer over gentle heat. Add pieces of the beurre manié until the sauce thickens, cover the casserole and continue cooking over a low heat OR place in a moderate oven, 350°F, until the chicken is tender – about 45-60 minutes.

Remove bay leaves and bouquet garni and garnish with fried bread croûtons and chopped parsley.

From the air Mont St-Michel (facing page) resembles an intricate fairy-tale sand castle.

Bateaux Mouches – sightseeing boats – offer a relaxing way of viewing the
delights of Paris from the River Seine.

SERVES 2-3

Fricassée of Guinea Fowl

Guinea fowl is very popular in France and often appears on restaurant menus. This simple recipe allows its full flavor to come through.

PREPARATION TIME: 30 minutes
COOKING TIME: 1 hour 30 minutes

1 guinea fowl	2 tbsps seasoned flour
4 slices bacon	2 cups water

Clean the guinea fowl and joint into pieces. Fry the bacon, coat the pieces of fowl with seasoned flour and fry until brown. Remove the bacon and fowl from the pan, add the flour and stir, slowly adding the water. Bring to the boil. Replace the fowl and bacon, cover and simmer until tender, about 1½ hours.

SERVES 4-6

Duck à l'Orange

A tangy fruity sauce perfectly complements the richness of duck and this orange sauce is one of the best-known in the repertoire.

PREPARATION TIME: 30 minutes
COOKING TIME: 15 minutes per lb, plus 15 minutes
20 minutes for the sauce

1 duck

ORANGE SAUCE
1 orange
⅔ cup water

1¼ cups Espagnole or brown sauce
1 tbsp lemon juice
2 tbsps port or claret

Place the duck in a greased roasting pan. Season. Lightly cover the duck with aluminum foil or double wax paper and place in the oven at 400°F. The duck should be basted frequently and the covering removed 20-30 minutes before the end of cooking time. After removing the covering, prick the breast all over to allow the extra fat to run out, leaving the breast crisp and succulent.

Orange sauce
Pare the rind from the orange, discarding any white pith. Cut the rind into wafer-thin strips and simmer these in water for about 10 minutes. Squeeze juice from the fruit. Strain the Espagnole or brown sauce, reheat with the orange rind, orange juice, lemon juice and wine. Serve the sauce with the cooked duck.

The Orangery (facing page) in the Palace of Versailles contained over 3,000 trees in its heyday, and is a testament to the determination of Louis XIV to live as extravagently as possible.

SERVES 4

Pigeon Ragout

In this tasty recipe the flavor of pigeon is greatly enhanced by the addition of red wine and pepper.

PREPARATION TIME: 30 minutes
COOKING TIME: 50-60 minutes

---

4 pigeons
½ tsp each cayenne, white and
     black pepper
2 tbsps oil
2 tbsps butter or margarine
12oz button onions
2 sticks celery, sliced
4 carrots, peeled and sliced
4 tbsps flour

1½ cups chicken stock
½ cup dry red wine
4oz button mushrooms, quartered
     or left whole if small
3oz fresh or frozen lima beans
2 tsps tomato paste (optional)
2 tbsps chopped parsley
Pinch salt

Wipe the pigeons with a damp cloth and season them inside the cavities with the three kinds of pepper and a pinch of salt.

Heat the oil in a heavy-based casserole and add the butter or margarine. Once it is foaming, place in the pigeons, two at a time if necessary, and brown them on all sides, turning them frequently. Remove from the casserole and set them aside.

To peel the button onions quickly, trim the root ends slightly and drop the onions into rapidly boiling water. Allow it to come back to the boil for about 1 minute. Transfer to cold water and leave to cool completely. The skins should come off easily. Trim roots completely. Add the onions, celery and carrots to the fat in the casserole and cook for about 5 minutes to brown slightly. Add the flour and cook until golden brown, stirring constantly. Pour in the stock and the wine and stir well. Bring to the boil over high heat until thickened. Stir in the tomato paste, if using, and return the pigeons to the casserole along with any liquid that has accumulated. Partially cover the casserole and simmer gently for about 40-45 minutes, or until the pigeons are tender. Add the mushrooms and lima beans halfway through the cooking time.

To serve, skim any excess fat from the surface of the sauce and sprinkle over the chopped parsley.

Part of the Queen's House in the rustic hamlet built by Louis XIV for his queen,
Marie Antoinette, at the Petit Trianon, Versailles.

SERVES 4-6

Gougère au Jambon

This savory pastry dish originated in Burgundy, but is also popular in the Champagne district and indeed in many other districts as well. Serve it as an appetizer or main course.

PREPARATION TIME: 30 minutes
COOKING TIME: 30-40 minutes for 1 large dish
15-20 minutes for individual dishes

CHOUX PASTRY
½ cup water
4 tbsps butter or margarine
½ cup all-purpose flour, sifted
2 eggs, beaten
½ cup cheese, finely diced
Pinch salt, pepper and dry mustard

HAM SALPICON
1 tbsp butter or margarine

1 tbsp flour
½ cup stock
2 tsps chopped fresh herbs
Salt and pepper
2oz mushrooms, sliced
4oz cooked ham, cut into julienne strips
2 tbsps shredded cheese and dry breadcrumbs mixed

Preheat oven to 400°F. Place the water for the pastry in a small saucepan. Cut the butter into small pieces and add to the water. Bring slowly to boil, making sure that the butter is completely melted before the water comes to a rapid boil. Turn up the heat and allow to boil rapidly for 30 seconds.

Sift the flour with a pinch of salt onto a sheet of paper. Take the pan off the heat and tip all the flour in at once. Stir quickly and vigorously until the mixture comes away from the sides of the pan. Spread onto a plate to cool.

Melt the butter in a small saucepan for the salpicon and add the flour. Cook for 1-2 minutes until pale straw colored. Gradually beat in the stock until smooth. Add a pinch of salt and pepper and the chopped herbs. Stir in the sliced mushrooms and ham and set aside.

To continue with the pastry, add salt, pepper and dry mustard to the paste and return it to the saucepan. Gradually add the egg to the paste mixture, beating well between each addition – this may be done by hand, with an electric mixer or in a food processor. It may not be necessary to add all the egg. The mixture should be smooth and shiny and hold its shape when ready. If it is still too thick, beat in the remaining egg. Stir in the diced cheese by hand.

Spoon the mixture into a large overproof pan or 4 individual dishes, pushing the mixture slightly up the sides of the dish and leaving a well in the center. Fill the center with the ham salpicon and scatter over 2 tbsps shredded cheese and dry breadcrumbs, mixed. Bake until the pastry is puffed and browned. Serve immediately.

The intricate wrought ironwork of the Eiffel Tower rising dramatically into the night sky above illuminated fountains.

SERVES 4-6

Ragoût d' Agneau

Serve this lamb casserole with French of garlic bread for a satisfying
supper dish

PREPARATION TIME: 30 minutes
COOKING TIME: 2¼ hours

1¼lbs boneless lamb shoulder or
leg or neck fillets cut in 2-inch
pieces
2lbs fresh tomatoes, peeled, seeded
and cut into large pieces, or the
same quantity canned
tomatoes, coarsely chopped and
juice reserved
1 bay leaf
1 clove garlic, minced
2 onions, cut in large pieces
12oz waxy potatoes, peeled and cut
in 2-inch pieces
¼ tsp cinnamon

Pinch ground cloves
Pinch nutmeg
Salt and pepper
4 tbsps red wine
1 eggplant cut in 1-inch pieces
6 zucchini, washed and cut into
2-inch pieces
4oz mushrooms, quartered
4 tbsps capers

Preheat oven to 350°F. Combine the lamb, tomatoes and reserved juice, bay leaf,
garlic, onions, potatoes, spices, salt and pepper in a casserole. Add the wine and stir. If
using fresh tomatoes, add about 1¼ cups water. Cover and cook in a moderate oven,
350°F, for 15 minutes. Check the amount of liquid and add water if necessary if the
stew becomes too dry. Cook a further 1 hour, uncovered, making sure the potatoes stay
submerged. Add the eggplant and cook for 30 minutes. 30 minutes before the end of
cooking, add the remaining ingredients. Skim any fat from the surface and remove the
bay leaf before serving.

The spotlit grandeur of the Arc de Triomphe by night.

SERVES 4

Navarin of Lamb Printanier

This is a dish in which to use the newest, freshest spring vegetables – hence its French name, for "printanier" means springlike.

PREPARATION TIME: 25 minutes
COOKING TIME: 1½ hours

2 tbsps oil
4 lamb chops
1 onion, sliced
2 cloves garlic, minced
4 tbsps flour
2½ cups stock
2 tbsps tomato paste
1 tsp fresh rosemary leaves
1 tsp fresh thyme

1½lbs of the following vegetables:
celery, cut in 2-inch pieces:
small new potatoes, scrubbed,
carrots, cut into thick barrel
shapes, small turnips, peeled
and trimmed, green beans, cut
into 2-inch pieces, small onions
or shallots, peeled, snow peas,
ends trimmed.

Heat the oil in a heatproof casserole. When the oil is hot, brown the chops on all sides and remove them to a plate and keep warm. Add the onion and garlic. Sauté for 2-3 minutes. Stir in the flour and allow to brown for 1-2 minutes. Gradually stir in the stock and add the tomato paste and herbs. Bring to the boil, stirring constantly. Replace the meat, cover and cook at 325°F for 45 minutes. Add the root vegetables such as potatoes, carrots, celery and turnips, stir well and cover and cook for 20-30 minutes or until meat and vegetables are tender. Add the green vegetables such as green beans and snow peas during the last 15 minutes of cooking. Skim any fat from the surface of the sauce and remove the bay leaf before serving.

Above: sunset over the River Seine in Paris – its soft reflection in the water giving the scene an almost Turneresque appearance.

SERVES 6

Rognons à la Dijonnaise

Veal kidneys are lighter in color and milder in flavor than lamb's kidneys.
Since they must be quickly cooked, kidneys make an ideal sauté dish.

PREPARATION TIME: 25 minutes
COOKING TIME: 15-17 minutes

¼ cup unsalted butter
3-4 whole veal kidneys
1-2 shallots, finely chopped
1 cup dry white wine
⅓ cup butter, softened

3 tbsps Dijon mustard
Salt, pepper and lemon juice to
   taste
2 tbsps chopped parsley

Melt the unsalted butter in a large sauté pan. Cut the kidneys into 1-inch pieces and
remove any fat or core. When the butter stops foaming, add the kidneys and sauté
them, uncovered, until they are light brown on all sides, about 10 minutes. Remove
the kidneys from the pan and keep them warm.

    Add the shallots to the pan and cook for about 1 minute, stirring frequently. Add
the wine and bring to the boil, stirring constantly and scraping the pan to remove any
browned juices. Allow to boil rapidly for 3-4 minutes until the wine is reduced to
about 3 tbsps. Remove the pan from the heat.

    Mix the remaining butter with the mustard, add salt and pepper and whisk the
mixture into the reduced sauce. Return the kidneys to the pan, add the lemon juice
and parsley and cook over low heat for 1-2 minutes to heat through. Serve
immediately.

The harbor at Audierne in Brittany – this region is famous for its fish and
seafood, and the town's restaurants serve the best of the catch.

SERVES 4-6

Filet de Porc aux Pruneaux

Tours, situated on the River Loire, is where this dish originated. It is a rich dish with its creamy sauce and wine-soaked prunes.

PREPARATION TIME: 25 minutes
COOKING TIME: 45 minutes

1lb pitted prunes	3 tbsps butter or margarine
2 cups white wine	1 tbsp redcurrant jelly
2-3 small pork tenderloins	1 cup heavy cream
1-2 tbsps flour	Salt and pepper

Soak the prunes in the white wine for about 1 hour and then put them into a very low oven to soften further. If the prunes are the ready-softened variety, soak for 20 minutes and omit the oven cooking.

Slice the pork fillet on the diagonal into 1-inch-thick pieces. Flatten them slightly with the palm of the hand. Dredge them with the flour, and melt the butter in a heavy pan. When the butter is foaming, put in the pork and cook until lightly browned on both sides. It may be necessary to cook the pork fillet in several batches.

Add half the soaking liquid from the prunes, cover the pan and cook very gently on moderate heat for about 45 minutes. If necessary, add more wine from the prunes while the pork is cooking.

When the pork is tender, pour liquid into a small saucepan and bring to the boil. Reduce by about ¼ and add the redcurrant jelly. Stir until dissolved and then add the cream. Bring the sauce back to the boil and allow to boil rapidly, stirring frequently. When the sauce is reduced and thickened slightly, pour over the meat and reheat. Add the prunes and transfer to a serving dish. Sprinkle with chopped parsley if desired.

Port le Val closely reflects the quiet beauty associated with Brittany, whose dramatic coastline makes it a favorite holiday destination for the French themselves.

SERVES 6

Roast Herbed Leg of Lamb

This is simple French cooking at its best – a delightful combination of fresh ingredients.

PREPARATION TIME: 15 minutes
COOKING TIME: 1¾ hours

3½lb leg of lamb
2-3 cloves garlic
2 bay leaves
½ cup polyunsaturated margarine

1½ cups breadcrumbs
1 tsp chopped fresh thyme
1 tsp chopped rosemary
1 tbsp chopped fresh parsley
Juice of 2 lemons
Freshly ground sea salt and black pepper

Prepare a sheet of foil large enough to wrap around the meat completely.

Peel and slice 1 or 2 of the garlic cloves. Make small cuts in the underside of the meat and insert the slices of garlic into this. Put the meat onto the foil with the bay leaves underneath. In a small bowl, mix the margarine thoroughly with the remaining ingredients. Spread this mixture over the upper surface of the meat, using a wetted palette knife. Loosely wrap the foil around the joint of meat, place in a roasting pan and roast in a preheated oven, 400°F, for about 1¾ hours.

Unwrap the foil and baste the meat with the melted fat that has collected in the base of the pan. Continue roasting, uncovered, for a further 30 minutes, until the crust is brown and crisp.

The fairy-tale splendor of Notre-Dame makes the visitor want to believe in the existence of Victor Hugo's fictional hunchback.

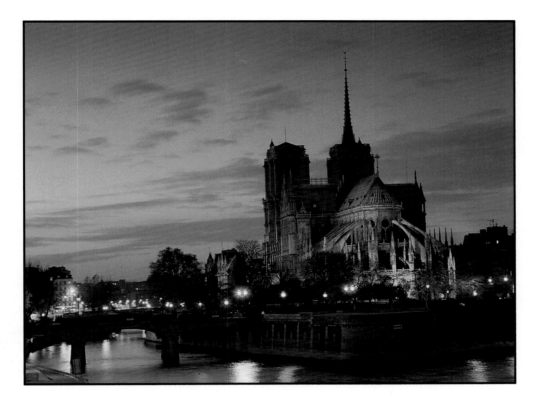

SERVES 6
Estouffade de Boeuf

A rich beef casserole with olives and mushrooms – perfect as a warming
winter dinner.

PREPARATION TIME: 10 minutes
COOKING TIME: 1 hour 40 minutes

2 tbsps olive oil
½lb smoked bacon, cubed
2¼lbs best braising steak, cut into
    smallish chunks
2 tbsps all-purpose flour
4 onions, sliced
Salt and pepper

1 bottle red wine
1 bouquet garni (with lots of
    thyme)
2 cloves garlic, chopped
1 cup mushrooms, sliced
½ cup pitted black olives

Heat 1 tbsp of the olive oil in a large, flameproof casserole and cook the bacon until the
juices run.

Roll the meat in the flour and shake off the excess. Add the meat to the casserole
with the bacon and the onions, and seal the meat on all sides. Skim off the excess fat.
Add salt and pepper and pour over the wine. Stir well, then allow to reduce over a
high heat, until about half the liquid remains. Add the bouquet garni and the garlic,
cover and cook in a moderate oven for 2 hours, checking and stirring from time to
time.

Sauté the mushrooms in the remaining olive oil. Strain the contents of the casserole
through a sieve, catching the juices in a clean saucepan. Put the meat and onions back
into the casserole and add the sautéed mushrooms. Put the juices back on the heat,
skim off any rising fat, then stir in the olives. Pour this sauce back over the contents of
the casserole and cook for a further 20 minutes. Remove the bouquet garni. Serve hot.

Paris by night is exciting and vibrant, offering Parisians and tourists alike the
chance to savor the city at its most romantic.

SERVES 4

Veal Jardinière

Jardin, French for garden, denotes a colorful garnish of vegetables, in this case a selection of carrots, beans, peas and tiny onions.

PREPARATION TIME: 25 minutes
COOKING TIME: 40 minutes

---

4 large veal chops
Oil for frying
1 tbsp butter or margarine
1 carrot, peeled and diced
12 button onions
1 tbsp flour

1½ cups beef stock
6 tbsps white wine
Salt and pepper
3oz green beans, topped, tailed
    and sliced
2oz peas

Heat about 2 tbsps of the oil in a large frying pan. Trim the chops to remove most of the fat. Fry on both sides in the hot fat until browned.

Melt the butter or margarine in a medium saucepan. Peel the onion and add to the butter with the carrot. Cook slowly to soften. Sprinkle on the flour and cook to a good golden brown. Add the stock, wine, salt and pepper and bring to the boil. Cook until thick. Pour the fat from the veal and pour in the sauce. Add the beans and peas and cook until the veal is tender, about 25 minutes.

The Eiffel Tower epitomizes Paris for many people, but when it was first opened in 1889, it was considered an eyesore.

SERVES 4

Noisettes Provençales

The tasty sauce in this recipe can be served with many plain broiled meats, to enliven them.

PREPARATION TIME: 40 minutes
COOKING TIME: 35 minutes

8 noisettes of lamb
¼ cup butter
1 tbsp oil

PROVENÇALE SAUCE
¼ cup butter
1 tbsp oil

1 large onion, finely chopped
1 clove garlic, minced
1lb tomatoes, skinned and
    chopped
1 tbsp tomato paste
⅔ cup dry white wine
Seasoning

Sauté the noisettes in the butter and oil for about 15 minutes, turning occasionally to brown the lamb on both sides.

    Meanwhile, heat the butter with the oil and add the onion and garlic. Fry gently until soft but not brown. Stir in the tomatoes, tomato paste and white wine, and bring to the boil, stirring continuously. Allow to cook uncovered over a fairly brisk heat for 10-15 minutes, stirring occasionally. Season to taste. Serve the sauce with the noisettes.

The Loire Valley is famous for its châteaux. Château Sully (right) has a fabulous light display in the evening which gives it an almost translucent quality.

SERVES 4

Steak au Poivre

This simple entrée dish is best served French style with crisp fries and a good green salad.

PREPARATION TIME: 15 minutes
COOKING TIME: 5-25 minutes

---

4 shell or fillet steaks	Salt
Oil	4 tbsps brandy
2 tbsps black hot peppers for steak	3 tbsps light cream
¼ cup butter	Watercress

Brush the steaks on both sides with oil, then coat with black hot peppers and crush these into the steak with a steak hammer. Melt the butter in a skillet and cook steaks for about 1½ minutes on each side. Reduce heat and cook for about a further minute for rare steak, 3 minutes for medium steak or 7 minutes if a well-done steak is required. Season with salt. Warm brandy in a ladle near the heat. Set it alight and pour over the steaks. Remove the steaks and place in a warmed serving dish. Keep hot. Stir the cream into the juices in the skillet. Heat gently for a few minutes. Pour sauce over steaks and garnish with watercress.

The chic resort of Cannes appears peaceful in the sunset, when the revelers have all retreated to the casinos and discos.

SERVES 4

Veal Marengo

The original of this dish contained chicken and was supposedly concocted
by Napoleon's chef after the battle of Marengo.

PREPARATION TIME: 30 minutes
COOKING TIME: 1 hour 20 minutes

1lb neck of veal
Seasoned flour
6 tbsps butter
2 onions, chopped
1¼ cups white stock
1 cup tomatoes, skinned and
 chopped
¼ cup mushrooms, chopped
Seasoning

GARNISH
4 slices of bread, cut into croûtons
Fat for frying
Parsley
Lemon

Cut the veal into cubes. Coat with seasoned flour and fry in butter until golden brown.
Add the onion and fry until transparent. Add the stock, tomatoes and mushrooms.
Season well. Simmer gently for about 1 hour. Serve garnished with the fried bread
croûtons, parsley and lemon.

The restaurants and cafés of Montmartre, in Paris, stay open long into the night
– though some times are busier than others!

SERVES 6

Soufflé au Citron Froid

A cold soufflé is really a mousse in disguise. It doesn't "rise" in the refrigerator, but is set above the rim of its dish with the help of a paper collar and gelatine.

PREPARATION TIME: 25-30 minutes

3 eggs, separated
¾ cup sugar
Grated rind and juice of 2 small
  lemons
1 tbsp gelatine dissolved in 3-4
  tbsps water
¾ cup heavy cream, lightly
  whipped

DECORATION
½ cup heavy cream, whipped
Thin strips lemon rind or lemon
  twists
Finely chopped almonds or
  pistachios

Tie a double thickness of wax paper around a soufflé dish to stand about 3 inches above the rim of the dish.

Beat the egg yolks in a large bowl until thick and lemon colored. Add the sugar gradually and then the lemon rind and juice. Set the bowl over a pan of hot water and whisk until the mixture is thick and leaves a ribbon-trail. Remove the bowl from the heat and whisk a few minutes longer. Melt the gelatine and the water until clear, pour into the lemon mixture and stir thoroughly. Set the bowl over ice and stir until beginning to thicken.

Whip the egg whites until stiff but not dry and fold into the lemon mixture along with the lightly whipped cream. Pour into the prepared soufflé dish and chill in the refrigerator until the gelatine sets completely. To serve, peel off the paper carefully and spread some of the cream on the sides of the mixture. Press finely chopped nuts into the cream. Pipe the remaining cream into rosettes on top of the soufflé and decorate with strips of lemon rind or lemon twists.

A peaceful, rural scene in the Picardy region of Northern France belies the area's turbulent past as the scene of some of the most famous battles of the First World War.

SERVES 6

French Apple Flan

A spectacular addition to the buffet table, French Apple Flan is typical of
the fruit tarts beloved by the French as a simple end to a good meal.

DOUGH
¾ cup all-purpose flour
¾ cup self-rising flour
¼ cup butter
¼ cup margarine
¼ cup confectioners' sugar
Cold water (about 2-3
    tablespoons)

FILLING
4 tbsps apricot jam
2 tbsps water
Juice of one small lemon
1¼lbs Bramley apples
1 tbsp confectioners' sugar

Preheat oven to 400°F.
    Place the flours in a bowl then cut in the fats until the mixture resembles fine
breadcrumbs. Stir in the confectioners' sugar. Mix to a firm but pliable dough with
cold water.
    Alternatively, sieve the flours into the bowl of a food processor, adding the fats in
small pieces. Process for 5 seconds. Add the confectioners' sugar and process for 2
seconds. Then, with the motor on, add cold water until all the ingredients form a
dough.
    Knead the dough lightly on a floured surface. Roll the pastry out and use to line a
9-9½-inch loose-bottomed French fluted flan tin.
    Boil together the jam and water for 2-3 minutes, stirring constantly. Sieve the glaze
into a cup to cool.
    Squeeze the lemon juice into a bowl. Peel, core and thinly slice the apples straight
into the lemon juice. Arrange the apple slices neatly in the pastry case. Sprinkle with
the sugar.
    Place the flan on a cookie sheet and cook in the preheated oven for approximately
35 minutes. Whilst still hot, brush the flan with the apricot glaze.
    Serve warm with whipping cream.

Villefranche is typical of the picturesque villages which make the Riviera so
popular.

SERVES 6

Tranche des Fruits

A spectacular dessert to make when summer fruits are cheap and plentiful.

14oz flaky pastry
Assorted fruit e.g. 2 kiwi, 2
   peaches, ¼lb cherries, small
   punnet strawberries, ¼lb grapes

3 tbsps apricot jam
1 tbsp lemon juice
Egg for glazing

Preheat oven to 425°F.

Roll out the pastry into a large rectangle approximately ⅓-inch thick. With a sharp knife, cut off strips from all sides 1-inch wide. Transfer the rectangle to a dampened cookie sheet and moisten the edges with cold water. Lay the strips along the edges making sure the strips are trimmed evenly, and press down lightly so both surfaces stick. Prick the base with a fork, leaving the edging strips plain. Flute or crimp the edges with a knife or finger and thumb. Glaze with a little beaten egg. Place the "tranche" into the preheated oven, prebake for 15-20 minutes, until risen and golden. Remove from the oven and cool on a wire rack.

Slice the peaches and kiwi fruit. Pit the cherries and pip the grapes and leave the strawberries whole. Place the fruit carefully in rows according to size or color. Meanwhile, put the jam into a small saucepan together with the lemon juice and bring to the boil, stirring continually. Allow to cool but not to reset. If it is too thick, add a little boiling water. Using a pastry brush, liberally coat the fruit with the jam glaze.

Do not make this dessert too long in advance – leave it as late as possible, not more than 1-3 hours before serving.

As an alternative, fill the base with 1 cup of crème patissière (pastry cream) or whipped heavy cream and top with fruit.

The French Alps offer some of the most spectacular scenery in France; it is
through these mountains that some of the most gruelling stages of the annual
Tour de France bicycle race take place.

Traditional Breton headresses, or *coiffes*, are still worn by some of the older
inhabitants of Brittany, and are part of the costume worn for the region's many
religious ceremonies which take place in the summer.

MAKES 1 pie

Tarte au Citron

A rich pâte sablée complements the tangy filling of this pie, found in
pâtisseries throughout France.

PREPARATION TIME: 1 hour, including chilling time
COOKING TIME: 30 minutes

PASTRY (PÂTE SABLÉE)
1¼ cups all-purpose flour
½ cup confectioners' sugar
A pinch of salt
½ cup butter
1 egg yolk
Few drops vanilla extract

FILLING
Finely grated rind and juice of 2
    large lemons
3 large eggs
¾ cup sugar
½ cup heavy cream

Preheat oven to 350°F.

Into a food processor, sift the flour, confectioners' sugar and salt. Add the butter cut
up into large dice. Process until the mixture resembles fine breadcrumbs. Stop and add
the egg yolk and vanilla extract. Process until the pastry forms a ball around the blade.
Do not process any longer. Chill the pastry for 30 minutes.

Roll out the pastry thinly on a floured board and line an 8-inch pie pan. Prebake in
the preheated oven for about 15 minutes. Remove and reduce heat to 300°F.

To make the filling, whisk together all the ingredients lightly and pour into the
pastry case. Return it to the cooled oven for another 15 minutes, or until the filling has
just set. Serve warm.

MAKES 12
Eclairs

Think of French pastry and eclairs immediately spring to mind.
French patisseries – pastry shops – sell them filled and iced in many
different flavors.

PREPARATION TIME: 40 minutes
COOKING TIME: 30-40 minutes

CHOUX PASTRY
⅞ cup water
⅓ cup butter or margarine
¾ cup all-purpose flour, sifted
3 eggs

CRÈME PATISSIÈRE
1 whole egg
1 egg yolk
¼ cup sugar

1 tbsp cornstarch
1½ tbsps flour
1 cup milk
Few drops vanilla extract

GLACÉ ICING
1lb confectioners' sugar
Hot water
Few drops vanilla extract

Preheat the oven to 350°F.
　　Combine the water and butter for pastry in a deep saucepan and bring to the boil. Once boiling rapidly, take the pan off the heat. Stir in the flour all at once and beat just until the mixture leaves the sides of the pan. Spread out onto a plate to cool. When cool, return to the saucepan and gradually add the beaten egg. Beat in well in between each addition of egg until the paste is smooth and shiny – should be of soft dropping consistency, but holding its shape well. It may not be necessary to add all the egg. Pipe or spoon into strips of about 3 inches long, spaced well apart on lightly-greased baking sheets. Sprinkle the sheets lightly with water and place in the oven. Immediately increase oven temperature to 375°F. Make sure the pastry is very crisp before removing it from the oven, this will take about 20-30 minutes cooking time. If the pastry is not crisp, return to the oven for a further 5 minutes.
　　To prepare the Crème Patissière, separate the whole egg and reserve the white. Mix the egg yolks and sugar together, sift in the flours and add about half the milk, stirring well. Bring the remainder of the milk to the boil and pour onto the yolk mixture, stirring constantly. Return the mixture to the pan and stir over heat until boiling point is reached. Take off the heat and whip the egg white until stiff but not dry. Fold the egg white into the mixture and return to the heat. Cook gently for about 1 minute, stirring occasionally. Add the vanilla extract at this point. Pour the mixture into a bowl and press a sheet of wax paper directly onto the surface of the crème and leave it to cool. Sift the confectioners' sugar into a bowl and add hot water, stirring constantly until the mixture is of thick coating consistency. The icing should cover the back of a wooden spoon but run off slowly. Add the vanilla extract.
　　To assemble the eclairs, cut the choux pastry almost in half lengthwise and either pipe or spoon in the Crème Patissière. Using a large spoon, coat the top of each eclair with a smooth layer of glacé icing. Allow the icing to set before serving.

MAKES 1 gâteau

Gâteau St Honoré

This is a fantasy choux pastry dessert. Also known as a corquembouche, it can be built directly onto a serving stand or onto a meringue or basic pastry base, and is a French favorite for weddings. If making the choux pastry a day in advance, the buns can be crisped by heating in a preheated oven at 350°F for 5 minutes. Cool before filling and assembling.

PREPARATION TIME: 1 hour 30 minutes
COOKING TIME: 30 minutes

CHOUX PASTRY
1 cup flour
Pinch of salt
6 tbsps butter
¾ cup water
3 beaten eggs

FILLING
2½ cups heavy cream
2 tbsps milk
2 tbsps sifted confectioners' sugar
2 tbsps raspberry liqueur

CARAMEL
1 cup granulated sugar
⅔ cup water

Sift the flour and salt together. Melt the butter in a heavy saucepan, with the water, and bring to the boil. Remove from heat. Add flour and salt mixture to the pan as soon as liquid has boiled. This should be carried out rapidly. Beat with a wooden spoon until glossy. The mixture should be of the right consistency to form small balls at this stage. Turn out onto a plate and spread out to cool. Return it to the pan and gradually beat in the eggs. Fill a pastry bag with the choux paste. Attach a ¾-inch plain nozzle. Pipe the choux paste into small balls on a greased cookie sheet. Make sure they are spaced well apart. Bake in the oven for 25 minutes until well risen and golden brown. They should be firm to touch. Pierce each bun to allow the steam to escape and return them to the oven for 2 minutes. Cool on a wire rack.

Filling
Whip half the cream with the milk, fold in the confectioners' sugar and the raspberry liqueur. Whip the remaining cream and use half to form a mound in the center of the serving plate or stand. With the other half, fill a pastry bag fitted with a star nozzle and reserve. Use the raspberry cream to fill another pastry bag fitted with a plain nozzle and fill each of the choux buns. Stick the choux buns round the cream mound so that it is completely covered and pipe rosettes between each bun using the plain cream.

For the caramel
Melt the sugar gently in a saucepan with the water and boil until it turns brown and caramalizes. Cool until the caramel begins to thicken but not set and pour quickly, but gently, over the gâteau. Leave to set and chill for ½ hour before serving.

MAKES 12 Crêpes

Crêpes Suzette

Possibly France's most famous dessert, crêpes suzette require last-minute cooking, but are much appreciated by guests.

PREPARATION TIME: 1 hour
COOKING TIME: 35 minutes

BATTER
1 cup flour
Pinch of salt or sugar (for extra sweetness)
1 egg, lightly beaten
1¼ cups milk
1 tsp vegetable oil

FILLING AND SAUCE
½ cup more sugar
5 tbsps butter
¾ cup fresh orange juice
6 lumps sugar
Rind of 1 orange
5 tbsps orange liqueur
3 tbsps brandy

Sieve the flour and salt into a bowl. Make a well in the center, break an egg into it and add half the milk. Beat well, then when smooth add the remaining milk. Leave the mixture to stand for 40 minutes. Grease a skillet and heat it a little. Pour the batter into the skillet. Quickly tilt and rotate the skillet so the batter coats the bottom and pour off any excess batter. Cook over a moderate heat until the underside of the crêpe is gently brown. Turn crêpe over and brown the other side. Turn onto wax paper and keep warm. Cook remaining batter in this way.

Cream the ½ cup sugar and the butter till fluffy. Beat in the orange juice and rub the sugar cubes onto the rind so they look orange. Set aside. Add the orange liqueur gradually. Spoon a little of the mixture into each crêpe and roll or fold. Put the remaining mixture into a large skillet and place the crêpes on top. Scatter the sugar cubes on the top. Gently heat the skillet and melt the butter. In another saucepan warm the brandy and pour over the pancakes. Ignite the brandy and serve.

The medieval bridge at Valentré spans the River Lot in the Dordogne, an area
which tempts the tourist with an abundance of tranquil, picturesque villages to
visit.

SERVES 6

Fresh Fruit Gratin

Fresh fruit, with a creamy topping, browned and crisped
under a hot broiler.

PREPARATION TIME: 25 minutes
COOKING TIME: 20 minutes

¾ cup confectioner's custard
2 tbsps kirsch
¾ cup whipping cream, whipped
   with ⅛ cup sugar

Seasonal fresh fruit, peeled, pitted,
   sliced or cubed (enough for 6
   servings)

Gently mix together the confectioner's custard, 2 tbsps whipped cream and the kirsch.
Using a metal spoon, gently fold in the remaining cream.

   Arrange the fruit in a pie pan, spoon over the topping and cook for 10 minutes in a
moderately hot oven. Transfer to a hot broiler, and allow the top to crisp until brown.
Serve immediately.

Left: part of the elegant, turn-of-the-century Pont Alexandre III which spans the
River Seine in Paris.

SERVES 6

Pears in Red Wine

Fruit desserts always make a refreshing end to a meal and this one is given
an elegant touch with a wine sauce.

PREPARATION TIME: 15 minutes, plus chilling time
COOKING TIME: 30 minutes

1½ cups granulated sugar
⅔ cup water

6 large pears, peeled
1 cup dry red wine

Gently heat the sugar and water until the sugar has dissolved. Add the pears and cover.
Then simmer for 15 minutes. Stir in the wine and continue to simmer uncovered for
another 15 minutes. Remove the pears from the saucepan and arrange in a serving
dish. Bring the wine syrup back to the boil and cook until thick. Pour over the pears
and allow to cool. Serve chilled.

Notre-Dame shimmers in the mellow light of early fall.

SERVES 4

Cremets

Nothing could be simpler than this dessert. It makes wonderful
summertime eating with fresh, soft fruits or a fruit compote.

PREPARATION TIME: 10 minutes

1½ cups curd cheese
2 tbsps vanilla sugar or superfine
    sugar with a few drops of vanilla
    essence
1¼ cups heavy cream

Beat the curd cheese until smooth. Add the sugar and gradually beat in the cream. Pile
into a bowl and chill.

Untouched by tourism, the harbor at Agde (facing page) gives a true picture of a
traditional fishing village.

SERVES 4-6

Mousse au Chocolat

Variations on this theme are endless – this one is lighter and less rich than some, but still deliciously chocolaty.

PREPARATION TIME: 20 minutes, plus chilling time

4oz semi-sweet chocolate,
    shredded
2½ tbsps water
1¼ tbsps instant coffee
4 egg whites
½ cup sugar

TO DECORATE
A little reserved chocolate,
    shredded

Put most of the chocolate, and the water and coffee into a bowl; stand it over a pan of hot water. Stir the mixture occasionally until the chocolate has melted and the mixture is smooth. Beat the egg whites until stiff but not dry, gradually beating in half the sugar. Mix the remaining sugar into the chocolate mixture and then fold in the meringue mixture. Divide the mousse between 4-6 glasses and sprinkle with the reserved chocolate. Chill briefly.

Barrage de Tignes, near the skiing resort of Val d'Isère. The area is popular
during the summer months, when the spectacular Alpine scenery, normally
hidden by winter snow, is fully revealed.

SERVES 6
Chestnut Parfait

Rich and luscious, this dessert is definitely for special occasions and not
for calorie-counters.

PREPARATION TIME: 40 minutes, plus freezing time

4 egg yolks
10 tbsps sugar
⅔ cup milk, warmed and flavored
  with a vanilla pod
14 tbsps unsweetened chestnut
  purée
2 tbsps dark rum

2 egg whites
¼ cup sugar
2 cups heavy cream
Chocolate leaves
A few cranberries
Whipped cream

Beat the egg yolks with the sugar and add the warmed milk flavored with the vanilla
pod and cook until thickened, stirring gently. The mixture should coat the spoon.
Transfer to a mixing bowl. Add the chestnut purée and the rum while the mixture is
still lukewarm. Chill well. Whip the egg whites with the sugar until very stiff. Beat the
cream until it peaks. Fold the egg white into the chestnut cream and carefully fold in
the whipped cream. Pour into a 6 cup mold and freeze for 4 hours. Decorate with small
rounds of sweetened chestnut purée dusted with chocolate powder or melted chocolate
sauce.

Rustic half-timbering in Normandy. The region is famed for its butter, cheese
and cream, and of course its Calvados – a delicious apple brandy.

MAKES 1 pie

French Plum Pudding

"Tarte Tatin" is a classic French apple dessert, cooked in this manner, but plums make a delicious alternative.

PREPARATION TIME: 20 minutes
COOKING TIME: 40 minutes

¾ cup all-purpose flour
¾ cup butter
6 tbsps superfine sugar
¼ cup ground almonds

1 egg yolk
1 tbsp cold water
1½lbs plums, halved and pitted

Preheat oven to 400°F.

Sift the flour into a mixing bowl. Cut in two thirds of the butter and 2 tbsps of the sugar. Add the ground almonds and mix into a firm dough with the egg yolk and water. Chill. Melt the remaining butter in a 9-inch round ovenproof dish. Add the remaining sugar until caramelized. Remove from heat. Arrange the plums, skin side down, in the ovenproof dish. On a lightly floured surface roll out the dough into a round slightly bigger than the dish. Place the dough on top of the plums and gently press down, tucking in the edges as you go. Bake in the preheated oven until golden. To serve, turn out onto a serving dish. Serve instantly.

A famous Paris landmark, the alabaster-white Sacré-Coeur Basilica (facing page) dominates the Montmartre district of Paris.

SERVES 4

Gateau Giennois

A nutty-flavored, fluffy-topped tart, with a surprise raspberry center.

PREPARATION TIME: 25 minutes
COOKING TIME: 25-35 minutes

1½ cups shortcrust pastry
3 egg yolks
½ cup sugar

3 tbsps shelled walnuts, ground
2 egg whites, stiffly beaten
4 tbsps raspberry jam

Roll out the pastry on a lightly floured surface. Line 4 individual pie pans with the pastry, pricking the base and sides with a fork.

Beat together the egg yolks and the sugar until white. Stir in the ground walnuts. Gently incorporate the beaten egg whites using a metal spoon. Place 1 tbsp of jam in the base of each tart and spoon over the mixture evenly between the 4 tarts.

Cook in a moderate oven 350°F until the pastry is cooked and the filling lightly puffed. Serve as soon as possible.

The fairy-tale château of Azay-le-Rideau is built partly over the River Indre and its glorious Renaissance architecture gives it a truly magical appearance.

INDEX